Jane.

CW01650813

# MATHS TODAY

## *for ages* 8 - 9

Addition

Subtraction

Multiplication

Division

Odd and Even Numbers

Length

Perimeter

Fractions

Time

Shape

Temperature

Handling Data

Number Sequences

Compass Directions

# Addition

Complete these additions as quickly as you can:

| a | b | c | d | e | f |
|---|---|---|---|---|---|
| 14 | 23 | 17 | 34 | 25 | 43 |
| + 12 | + 15 | + 2 | + 14 | + 24 | + 21 |
| ____ | ____ | ____ | ____ | ____ | ____ |

Minnie

Sometimes it is best to add numbers together in your head, but if you write them down you should always write the figures in the correct columns.

These figures are in the tens column.

These figures are in the units column.

```
  2 3
+ 1 4
```

Max

When we are writing sums down, we add the units figures first then we add the tens figures.

Step One: add the units first

```
  2 3
+ 1 4
-----
    7
```

three units add four units make seven units.

Step Two: add the tens

```
  2 3
+ 1 4
-----
  3 7
```

two tens add one ten make three tens.

Twenty-three add fourteen equals thirty-seven.

Complete these additions. Remember to add the units first.

| g | h | i | j | k | l |
|---|---|---|---|---|---|
| 23 | 35 | 64 | 75 | 54 | 56 |
| + 16 | + 12 | + 23 | + 14 | + 24 | + 42 |
| ____ | ____ | ____ | ____ | ____ | ____ |

```
  38
+ 25
----

----
```

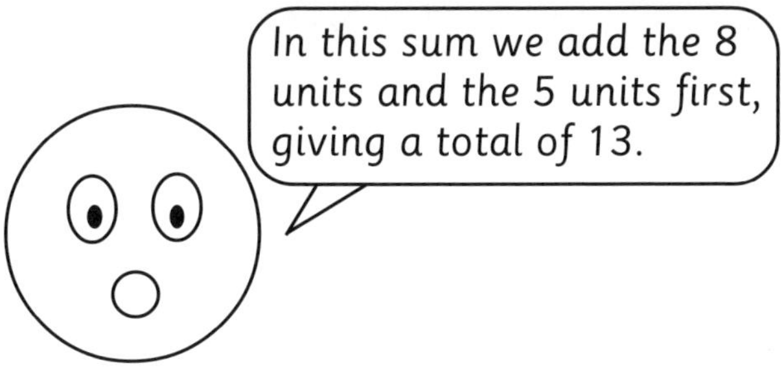


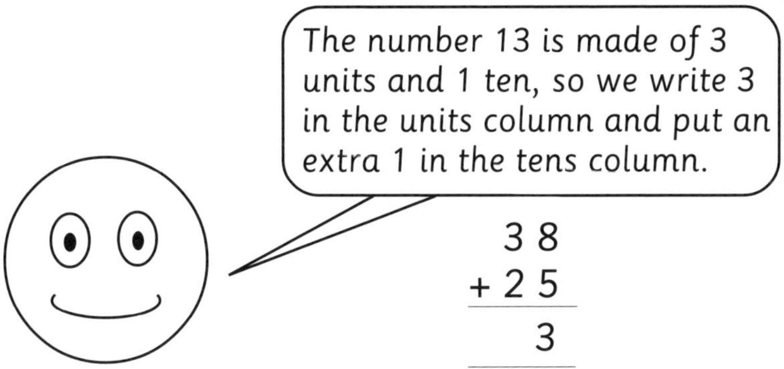


```
  38
+ 25
----
   3
----
  1
```

Now we add up the three tens, the two tens and the one extra ten:

```
  38
+ 25
----
  63
----
  1
```

Complete these additions.

Remember: there are not always enough units to make an extra ten.

| | | | |
|---|---|---|---|
| (a) 36 + 25 = ____ | (b) 55 + 28 = ____ | (c) 47 + 14 = ____ | (d) 52 + 37 = ____ |
| (e) 48 + 36 = ____ | (f) 54 + 14 = ____ | (g) 67 + 9 = ____ | (h) 78 + 17 = ____ |

## Mental Speed

How quickly can you answer these questions?
Time yourself and record your score.

1) 4 + 7 =
2) 5 + 9 =
3) 8 + 7 =
4) 6 + 5 =
5) 7 + 7 =
6) 4 + 8 =
7) 9 + 4 =
8) 6 + 8 =
9) 9 + 8 =
10) 8 + 5 =
11) 7 + 6 =
12) 3 + 9 =
13) 9 + 9 =
14) 7 + 8 =
15) 6 + 7 =
16) 5 + 7 =
17) 8 + 3 =
18) 8 + 8 =
19) 6 + 6 =
20) 7 + 3 =

Time taken:

☐ minutes and

☐ seconds.

# More Addition

Sometimes sums are written like this: 47 + 18 =

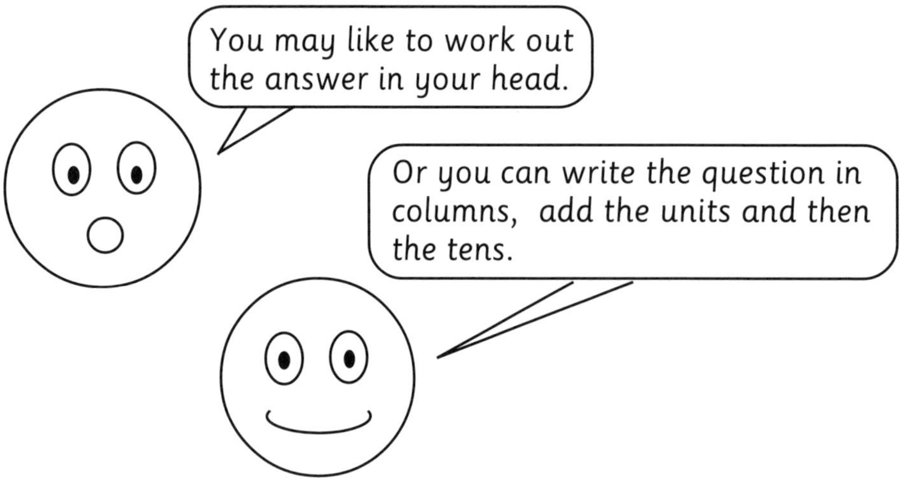


```
  47
+ 18
____

____
```

Always make sure that you write the figures in the correct columns.

(a) 28 + 17

```
  28
+ 17
____

____
```

(b) 49 + 8

```
  49
+  8
____

____
```

(c) 24 + 36

```
____

____
```

(d) 53 + 9

```
____

____
```

(e) In Class 1 there are 31 children and in Class 2 there are 32 children. How many children are there altogether in the two classes?

```
  31
+ 32
____

____
```

(f) There are 47 apple trees in one orchard and 38 apple trees in another orchard. How many apple trees are there altogether?

```
____

____
```

(g) 68 cartons of milk are delivered in South Street and 32 are delivered in North Street. How many cartons of milk are delivered altogether?

```
____

____
```

# Hundreds, Tens and Units Addition

346 + 37

```
  346
+  37
  ---
  383
   1
```

Notice how the figures are in the correct columns in this question and its answer.

(a) 214 + 168

(b) 529 + 59

(c) 577 + 321

(d) 745 + 235

(e) 400 + 397

(f) 367 + 28

(g) 750 + 139

(h) 418 + 8

(i) 808 + 149

## Mental Speed

How quickly can you answer these questions?
Time yourself and record your score.

1) 12 + 7 =

2) 15 + 4 =

3) 8 + 17 =

4) 13 + 6 =

5) 24 + 4 =

6) 3 + 12 =

7) 14 + 14 =

8) 16 + 12 =

9) 7 + 9 =

10) 13 + 5 =

11) 6 + 14 =

12) 9 + 13 =

13) 11 + 11 =

14) 12 + 12 =

15) 13 + 13 =

16) 17 + 7 =

17) 9 + 15 =

18) 16 + 14 =

19) 3 + 28 =

20) 5 + 25 =

Time taken:

☐ minutes and

☐ seconds.

# Subtraction

For example, to subtract 32 from 47 you could make jumps on a number line:

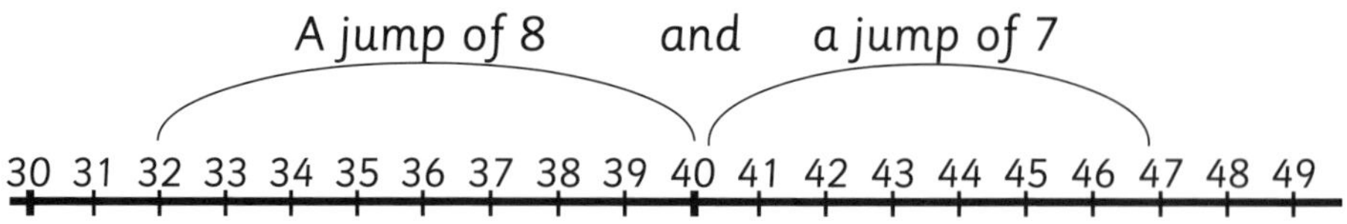


... so we've jumped 15 altogether: 47 – 32 = 15

**Step One:** subtract the units first

```
  47
- 32
----
   5
```

seven units subtract two units make five units.

**Step Two:** subtract the tens

```
  47
- 32
----
  15
```

four tens subtract three tens make one ten.

Forty-seven subtract thirty-two equals fifteen    47 – 32 = 15

| | | | | | |
|---|---|---|---|---|---|
| (a) 24 - 13 = ____ | (b) 28 - 15 = ____ | (c) 17 - 5 = ____ | (d) 65 - 23 = ____ | (e) 76 - 24 = ____ | (f) 83 - 61 = ____ |
| (g) 36 - 12 = ____ | (h) 47 - 23 = ____ | (i) 25 - 14 = ____ | (j) 63 - 21 = ____ | (k) 87 - 24 = ____ | (l) 78 - 46 = ____ |
| (m) 89 - 76 = ____ | (n) 57 - 21 = ____ | (o) 98 - 62 = ____ | (p) 79 - 25 = ____ | (q) 68 - 57 = ____ | (r) 99 - 24 = ____ |

```
  4 3
- 2 5
-----

-----
```

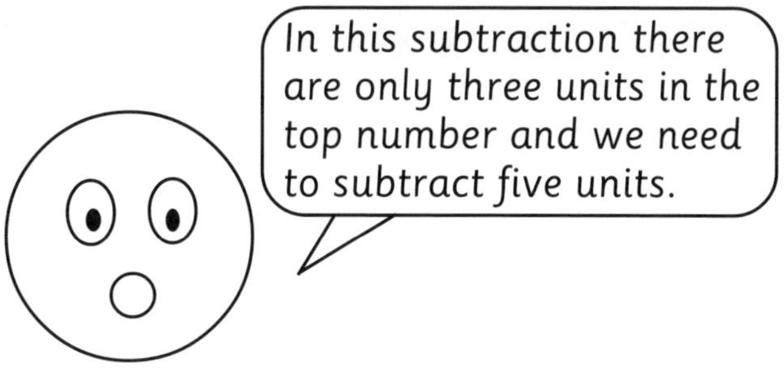


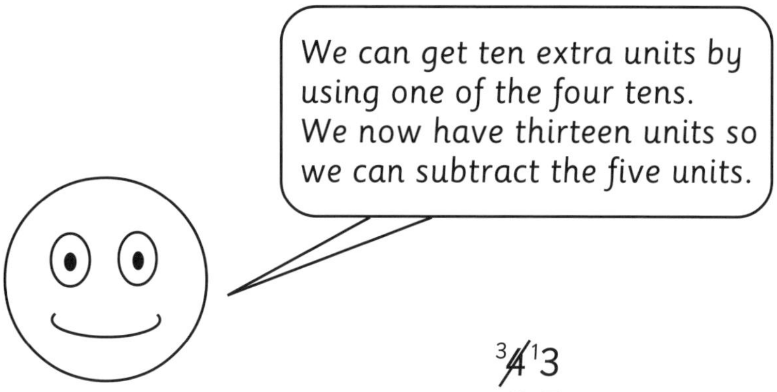


$$\begin{array}{r} {}^{3}\not{4}\,{}^{1}3 \\ -\ 2\ 5 \\ \hline 8 \\ \hline \end{array}$$

Now we subtract the two tens from the three tens we have left:

$$\begin{array}{r} {}^{3}\not{4}\,{}^{1}3 \\ -\ 2\ 5 \\ \hline 1\ 8 \\ \hline \end{array}$$

Complete these subtractions. Remember: we do not always need to get extra units from one of the tens.

| | | | |
|---|---|---|---|
| (a) 45 - 17 = ____ | (b) 63 - 37 = ____ | (c) 72 - 57 = ____ | (d) 85 - 42 = ____ |
| (e) 74 - 46 = ____ | (f) 92 - 58 = ____ | (g) 67 - 9 = ____ | (h) 91 - 64 = ____ |

## Mental Speed

How quickly can you answer these questions?
Time yourself and record your score.

1) 11 - 7 =

2) 9 - 5 =

3) 13 - 8 =

4) 8 - 2 =

5) 18 - 9 =

6) 7 - 4 =

7) 17 - 9 =

8) 6 - 1 =

9) 15 - 8 =

10) 9 - 4 =

11) 16 - 7 =

12) 8 - 3 =

13) 14 - 9 =

14) 7 - 5 =

15) 13 - 6 =

16) 7 - 3 =

17) 11 - 6 =

18) 12 - 8 =

19) 9 - 7 =

20) 14 - 6 =

Time taken:

☐ minutes and

☐ seconds.

# More Subtraction

Sometimes subtractions are written like this: 56 – 29 =

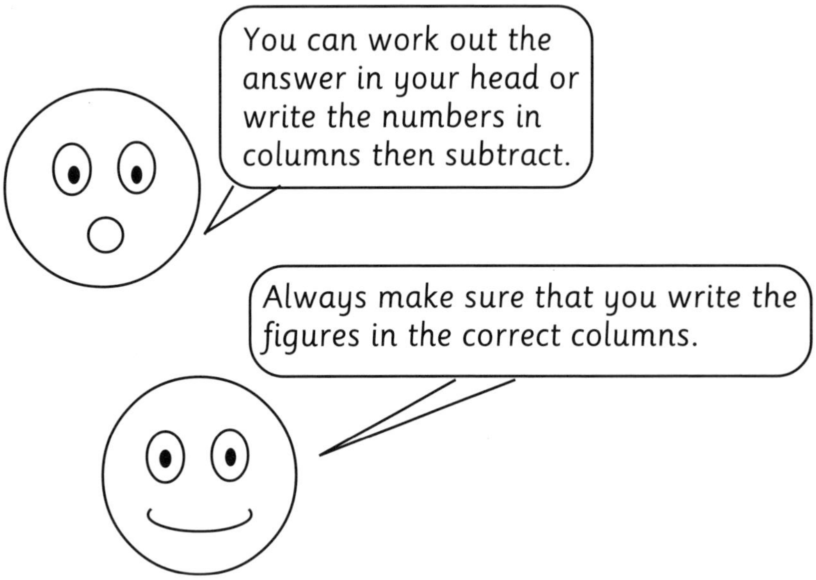


```
  56
- 29
____

____
```

(a) 49 – 22

```
  49
- 22
____

____
```

(b) 47 – 8

```
  47
-  8
____

____
```

(c) 86 – 42

```
____

____
```

(d) 72 – 39

```
____

____
```

(e) There are 85 children in Ford Village School and 59 children in Westland School. How many more children are there in Ford School?

```
  85
- 59
____

____
```

(f) There are 93 cows on Home Farm. The farmer sells 28 of the cows. How many cows has he got left?

```
____

____
```

(g) 68 cartons of milk are delivered in South Street and 32 are delivered in North Street. How many more cartons of milk are delivered in South Street than in North Street?

```
____

____
```

# Hundreds, Tens and Units Subtraction

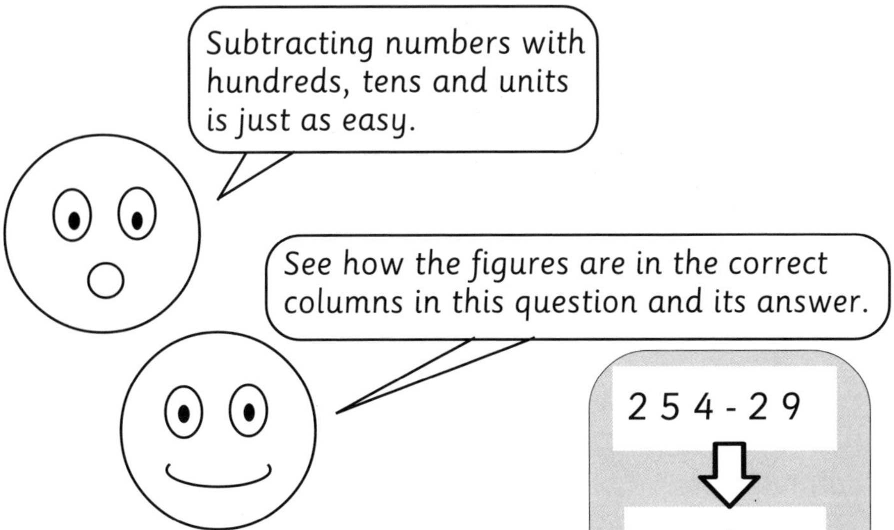


254 - 29

```
   4 1
  2 5 4
-   2 9
  2 2 5
```

(a) 347 - 108

(b) 659 - 235

(c) 738 - 29

(d) 982 - 167

(e) 874 - 49

(f) 479 - 218

(g) 653 - 28

(h) 911 - 7

(i) 391 - 146

## Mental Speed

How quickly can you answer these questions?
Time yourself and record your score.

1) 23 - 7 =

2) 32 - 6 =

3) 17 - 6 =

4) 19 - 7 =

5) 22 - 4 =

6) 25 - 12 =

7) 18 - 9 =

8) 20 - 8 =

9) 20 - 6 =

10) 20 - 4 =

11) 30 - 4 =

12) 30 - 5 =

13) 30 - 7 =

14) 30 - 17 =

15) 40 - 8 =

16) 40 - 2 =

17) 40 - 6 =

18) 40 - 9 =

19) 50 - 5 =

20) 50 - 1 =

Time taken:

☐ minutes and

☐ seconds.

# Odds and Evens

2 4 6 8 10

1 3 5 7 9

Are these numbers odd or even?

| | | | | | |
|---|---|---|---|---|---|
| (a) 7 | (b) 3 | (c) 6 | (d) 9 | (e) 8 | (f) 2 |
| ______ | ______ | ______ | ______ | ______ | ______ |

Is this number odd or even? 347

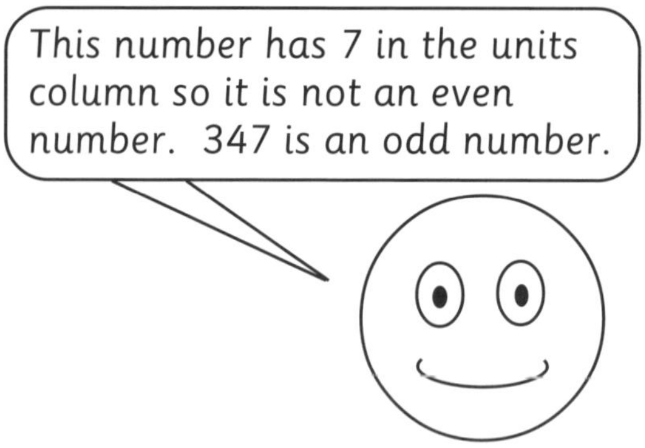


Are these numbers odd or even?

| | | | | | |
|---|---|---|---|---|---|
| (g) 234 | (h) 1679 | (i) 800 | (j) 58 | (k) 31 | (l) 999 |
| ______ | ______ | ______ | ______ | ______ | ______ |

# Numbers to words

Match the numbers to the words:

| | | |
|---|---|---|
| a | 23 | three hundred and forty |
| b | 1216 | six hundred and eighty-two |
| c | 340 | two thousand, seven hundred and two |
| d | 999 | twenty-three |
| e | 2702 | nine hundred and ninety-nine |
| f | 682 | one thousand, two hundred and sixteen |

Re-write these lists of numbers in order.
Start with the smallest.

| | | | | | |
|---|---|---|---|---|---|
| g | 725 | 318 | 57 | 796 | 100 |
| | ______ | ______ | ______ | ______ | ______ |
| h | 48 | 3497 | 616 | 9000 | 276 |
| | ______ | ______ | ______ | ______ | ______ |

Thousands
Hundreds
Tens
Units

3,496

Write these numbers in figures:

| | | |
|---|---|---|
| i | four thousand, six hundred and ten | |
| j | five hundred and fifty-four | |
| k | six thousand, two hundred and eighty-one | |
| l | one thousand and one | |

## Mental Speed

How quickly can you answer these questions?
Time yourself and record your score.

1) 8 + 6 =
2) 14 - 6 =
3) 14 + 6 =
4) 20 - 6 =
5) 20 - 3 =
6) 20 - 9 =
7) 20 - 2 =
8) 20 - 8 =
9) 20 - 4 =
10) 20 - 1 =
11) 20 - 5 =
12) 20 - 7 =
13) 13 + 7 =
14) 16 + 4 =
15) 12 + 8 =
16) 7 + 5 =
17) 9 + 8 =
18) 12 - 5 =
19) 17 - 9 =
20) 17 - 8 =

Time taken:

☐ minutes and

☐ seconds.

# Measurement of length

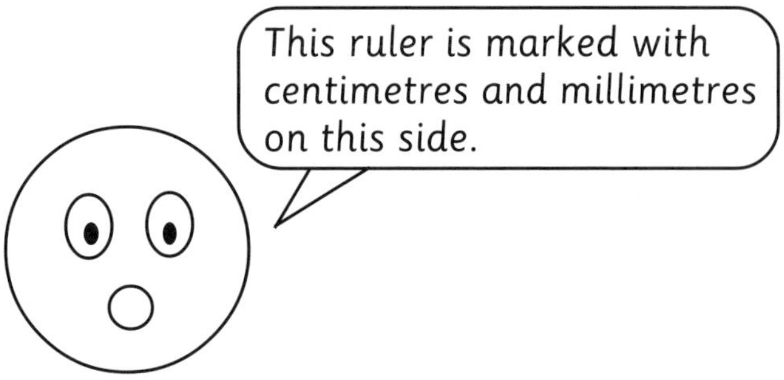


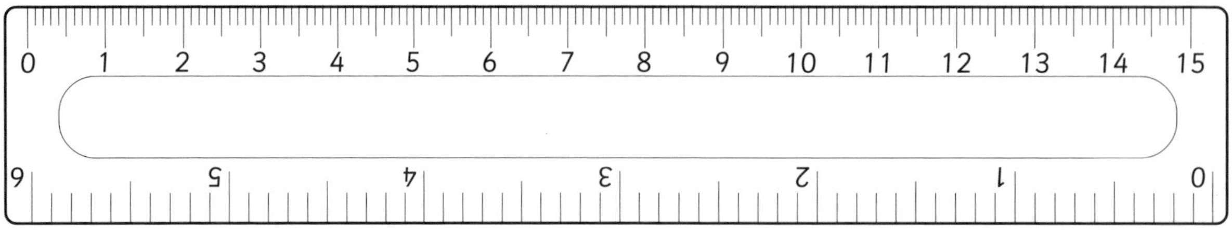

We can use the ruler to measure the length of this black line:

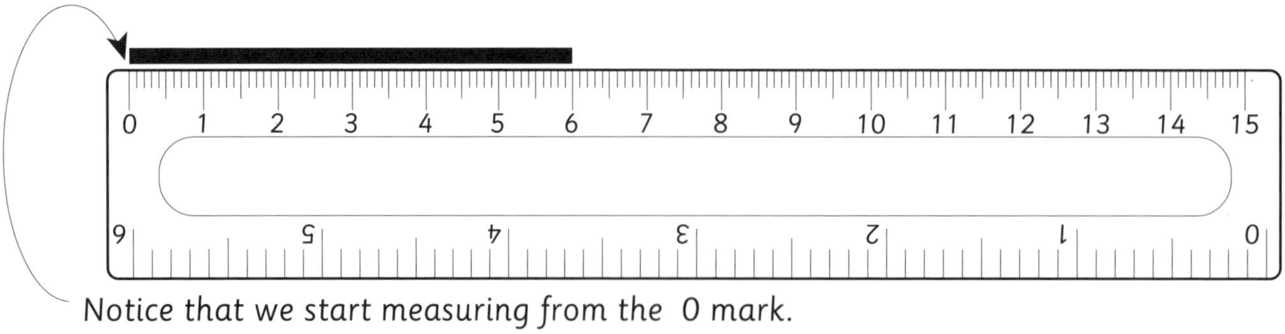

Notice that we start measuring from the 0 mark.

The black line is 6 centimetres long. We can write 6 centimetres like this: 6 cm

This line measures 9 centimetres and 7 millimetres.

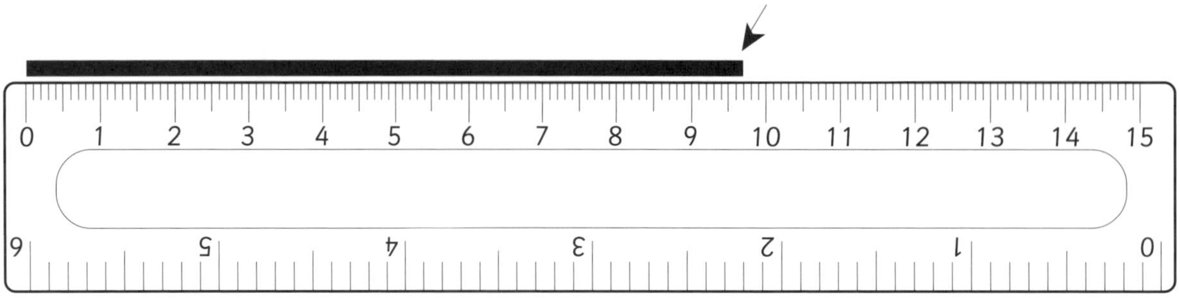

We can write 9 centimetres and 7 millimetres like this: 9 cm 7 mm

Use your ruler to measure the lines below:

(a)

cm mm

(b)

cm

(c)

cm mm

(d)

cm mm

(e)

cm

Use your ruler to measure the lines below.
Remember to write cm or cm mm .

(f)

(g)

(h)

(i)

## Mental Speed

How quickly can you answer these questions?
Time yourself and record your score.

1) 20 + 10 =

2) 50 + 20 =

3) 30 + 30 =

4) 70 + 20 =

5) 10 + 60 =

6) 40 + 30 =

7) 60 + 30 =

8) 80 + 10 =

9) 20 + 60 =

10) 50 + 40 =

11) 30 + 50 =

12) 70 + 10 =

13) 10 + 40 =

14) 40 + 60 =

15) 60 + 10 =

16) 80 + 20 =

17) 10 + 18 =

18) 40 + 23 =

19) 60 + 35 =

20) 80 + 14 =

Time taken:

minutes and

seconds.

# Measuring Perimeter

Use your ruler to measure each side of the rectangle. Write the measurements in the boxes.

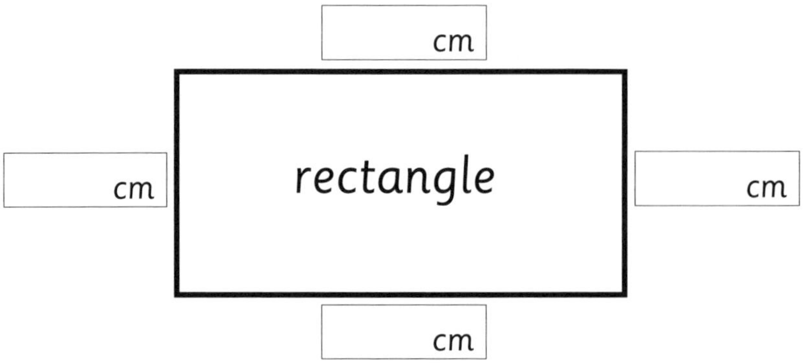


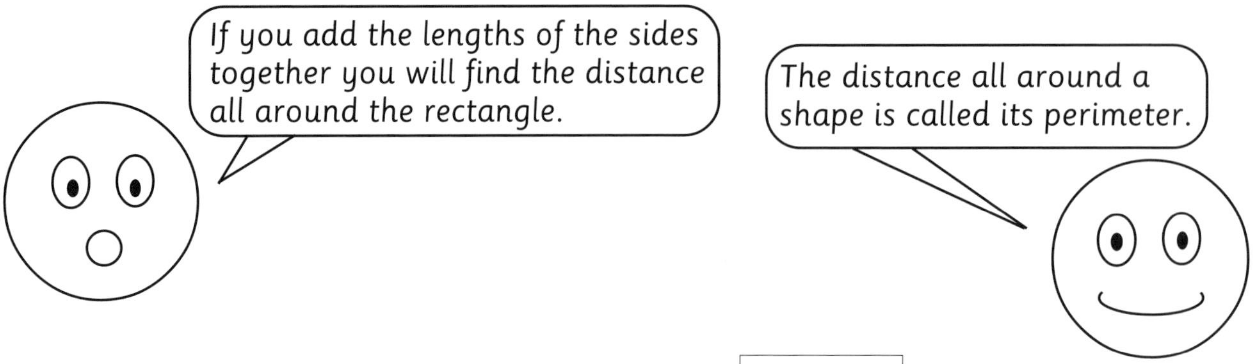


The perimeter of the rectangle is ______ cm.

Measure the sides of the shapes below and then find the perimeter of each one.

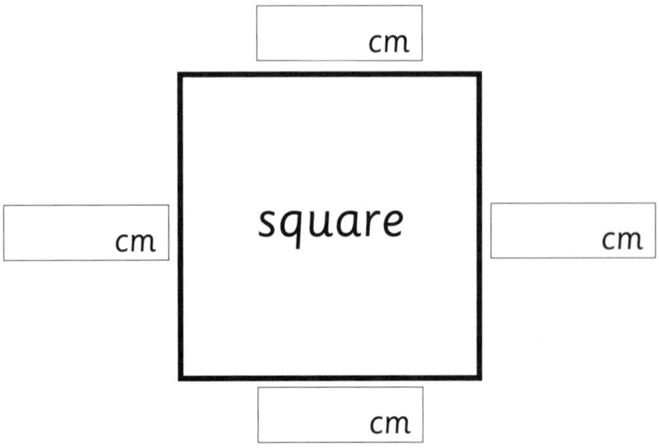


The perimeter of the square is ______ cm

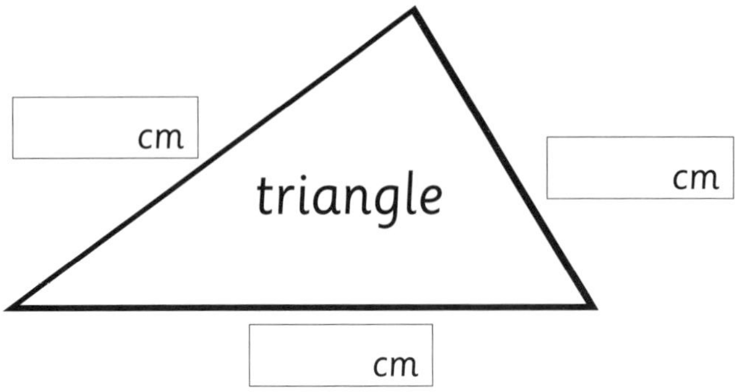


The perimeter of the triangle is ______ cm

# More shapes

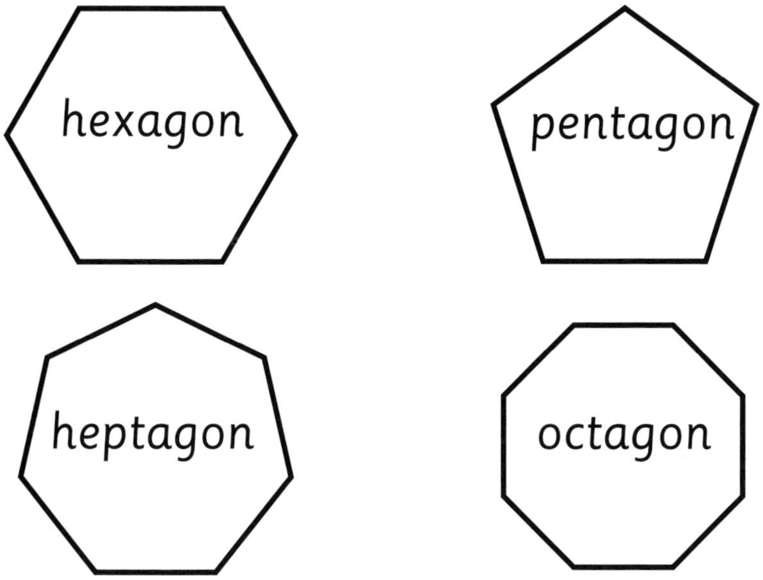


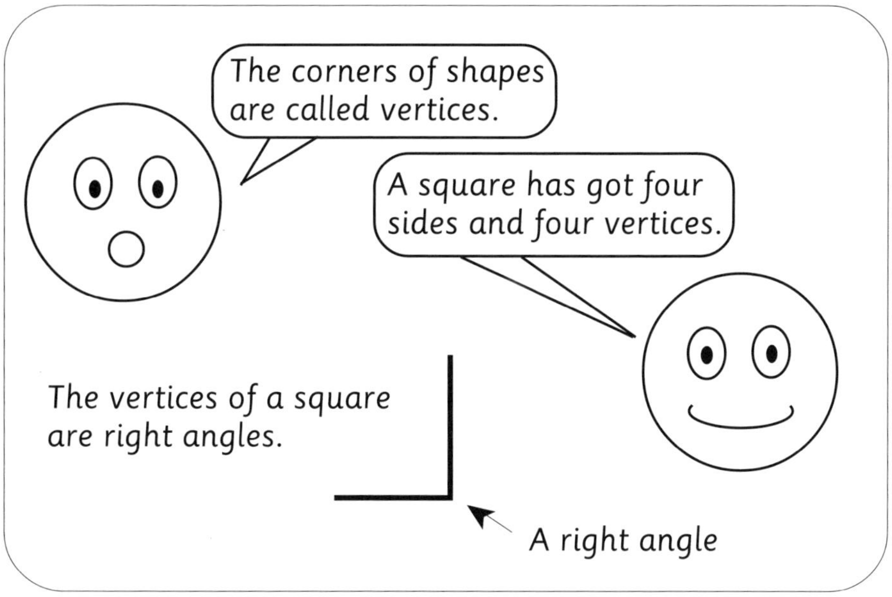


Fill in the gaps in this chart:

| shape | number of sides | number of vertices |
|---|---|---|
| square | 4 | |
| rectangle | | |
| hexagon | | |
| | | 5 |
| | 7 | |
| octagon | | |

## Mental Speed

How quickly can you answer these questions?
Time yourself and record your score.

1) 20 - 10 =
2) 50 - 20 =
3) 30 - 30 =
4) 70 - 20 =
5) 60 - 10 =
6) 40 - 30 =
7) 60 - 30 =
8) 80 - 10 =
9) 90 - 20 =
10) 80 - 40 =
11) 90 - 50 =
12) 70 - 10 =
13) 80 - 40 =
14) 90 - 60 =
15) 60 - 20 =
16) 80 - 20 =
17) 80 - 21 =
18) 40 - 3 =
19) 60 - 5 =
20) 80 - 4 =

Time taken:

☐ minutes and

☐ seconds.

# Multiplication

Fill in the missing answers in these multiplication tables. You can count on with your fingers to help you.

| two times table |
|---|
| 1 x 2 = 2 |
| 2 x 2 = |
| 3 x 2 = 6 |
| 4 x 2 = 8 |
| 5 x 2 = 10 |
| 6 x 2 = |
| 7 x 2 = 14 |
| 8 x 2 = |
| 9 x 2 = 18 |
| 10 x 2 = |

| three times table |
|---|
| 1 x 3 = 3 |
| 2 x 3 = 6 |
| 3 x 3 = |
| 4 x 3 = 12 |
| 5 x 3 = |
| 6 x 3 = 18 |
| 7 x 3 = 21 |
| 8 x 3 = |
| 9 x 3 = 27 |
| 10 x 3 = |

| four times table |
|---|
| 1 x 4 = 4 |
| 2 x 4 = |
| 3 x 4 = 12 |
| 4 x 4 = 16 |
| 5 x 4 = |
| 6 x 4 = 24 |
| 7 x 4 = |
| 8 x 4 = 32 |
| 9 x 4 = |
| 10 x 4 = 40 |

| five times table |
|---|
| 1 x 5 = |
| 2 x 5 = 10 |
| 3 x 5 = 15 |
| 4 x 5 = |
| 5 x 5 = |
| 6 x 5 = 30 |
| 7 x 5 = |
| 8 x 5 = |
| 9 x 5 = 45 |
| 10 x 5 = |

| six times table |
|---|
| 1 x 6 = 6 |
| 2 x 6 = |
| 3 x 6 = 18 |
| 4 x 6 = |
| 5 x 6 = 30 |
| 6 x 6 = |
| 7 x 6 = 42 |
| 8 x 6 = |
| 9 x 6 = 54 |
| 10 x 6 = |

| seven times table |
|---|
| 1 x 7 = |
| 2 x 7 = 14 |
| 3 x 7 = |
| 4 x 7 = 28 |
| 5 x 7 = |
| 6 x 7 = 42 |
| 7 x 7 = |
| 8 x 7 = 56 |
| 9 x 7 = |
| 10 x 7 = 70 |

| eight times table |
|---|
| 1 x 8 = 8 |
| 2 x 8 = |
| 3 x 8 = 24 |
| 4 x 8 = |
| 5 x 8 = 40 |
| 6 x 8 = |
| 7 x 8 = 56 |
| 8 x 8 = |
| 9 x 8 = 72 |
| 10 x 8 = |

| nine times table |
|---|
| 1 x 9 = |
| 2 x 9 = 18 |
| 3 x 9 = 27 |
| 4 x 9 = |
| 5 x 9 = |
| 6 x 9 = 54 |
| 7 x 9 = |
| 8 x 9 = |
| 9 x 9 = 81 |
| 10 x 9 = |

| ten times table |
|---|
| 1 x 10 = 10 |
| 2 x 10 = |
| 3 x 10 = 30 |
| 4 x 10 = |
| 5 x 10 = 50 |
| 6 x 10 = |
| 7 x 10 = 70 |
| 8 x 10 = |
| 9 x 10 = 90 |
| 10 x 10 = 100 |

## Mental Speed

How quickly can you answer these questions?
Time yourself and record your score.

1) 10 x 10 =
2) 6 x 7 =
3) 4 x 5 =
4) 9 x 3 =
5) 8 x 4 =
6) 7 x 6 =
7) 3 x 8 =
8) 5 x 9 =
9) 8 x 7 =
10) 10 x 6 =
11) 5 x 4 =
12) 7 x 9 =
13) 2 x 8 =
14) 4 x 6 =
15) 9 x 8 =
16) 3 x 6 =
17) 8 x 8 =
18) 6 x 9 =
19) 2 x 7 =
20) 10 x 4 =

Time taken:

☐ minutes and

☐ seconds.

# More multiplication

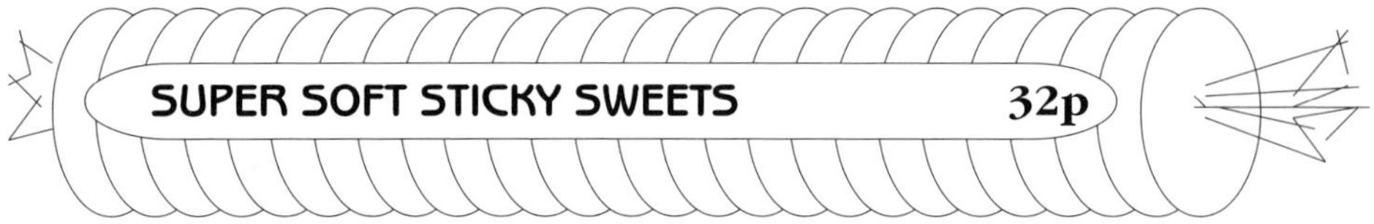


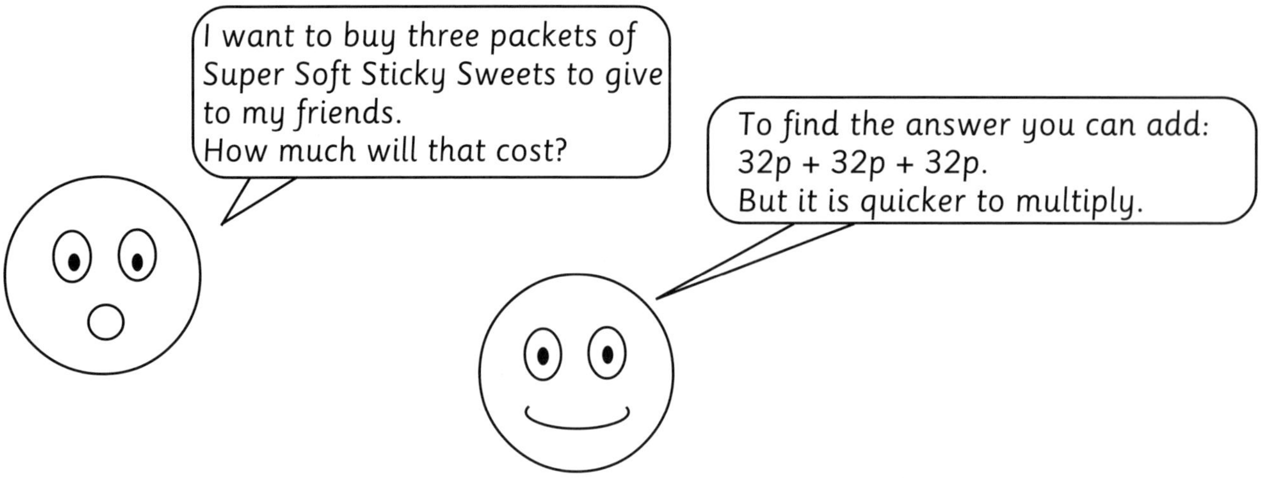


Step One:
multiply the two units by three

$$\begin{array}{r} 32 \\ \times\ \ 3 \\ \hline 6 \\ \hline \end{array}$$

three times two is six.

Step Two:
multiply the three tens by three

$$\begin{array}{r} 32 \\ \times\ \ 3 \\ \hline 96 \\ \hline \end{array}$$

three times three is 9.

Three times thirty-two equals ninety-six.

So the 3 packets of sweets will cost 96p.

Complete these multiplications.

| a | b | c | d | e | f |
|---|---|---|---|---|---|
| 14 × 2 | 23 × 3 | 12 × 4 | 31 × 2 | 24 × 2 | 43 × 2 |

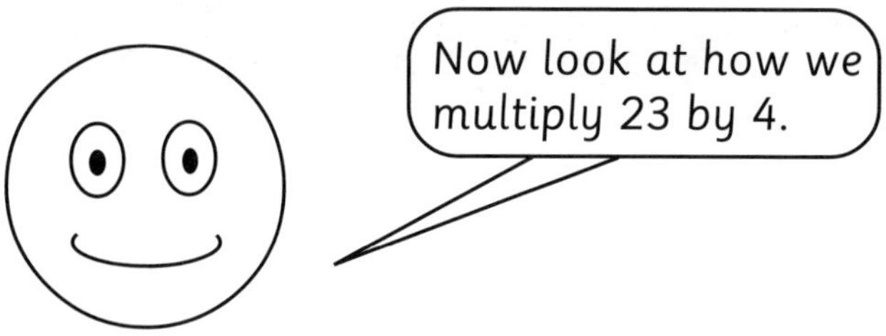


Step One:
multiply the three units by four

$$\begin{array}{r} 23 \\ \times\ \ 4 \\ \hline 2 \\ \hline {\scriptstyle 1\ \ } \end{array}$$

*four times three is twelve so we write 2 in the units and put 1 in the tens.*

Step Two:
multiply the two tens by four

$$\begin{array}{r} 23 \\ \times\ \ 4 \\ \hline 92 \\ \hline {\scriptstyle 1\ \ } \end{array}$$

*four times 2 tens is 8 tens but don't forget to add the extra 1 ten to make 9 tens.*

Four times twenty-three equals ninety-two.

Complete these multiplications.

Remember:

There are not always enough units to make extra tens.

| | | | |
|---|---|---|---|
| (a) $36 \times 2$ = ____ | (b) $15 \times 3$ = ____ | (c) $27 \times 2$ = ____ | (d) $17 \times 5$ = ____ |
| (e) $14 \times 5$ = ____ | (f) $34 \times 2$ = ____ | (g) $24 \times 4$ = ____ | (h) $46 \times 2$ = ____ |

## Mental Speed

How quickly can you answer these questions?
Time yourself and record your score.

1) 3 x 10 =
2) 5 x 7 =
3) 4 x 9 =
4) 9 x 8 =
5) 7 x 4 =
6) 7 x 9 =
7) 6 x 8 =
8) 5 x 3 =
9) 2 x 7 =
10) 10 x 9 =
11) 8 x 4 =
12) 7 x 7 =
13) 5 x 8 =
14) 4 x 8 =
15) 6 x 6 =
16) 5 x 6 =
17) 8 x 7 =
18) 5 x 9 =
19) 2 x 4 =
20) 10 x 7 =

Time taken:
☐ minutes and
☐ seconds.

# Temperature

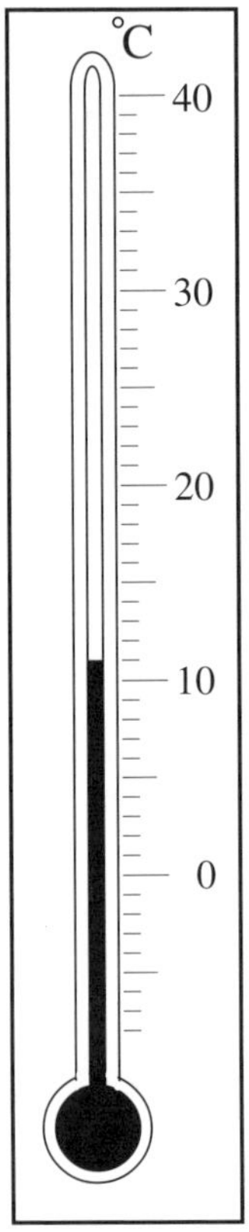

We use a thermometer to measure temperature.

We measure temperature in degrees Celsius.

The little circle means degrees.

Degrees Celsius can be written like this: °C

The temperature on this thermometer is 11 degrees Celsius.

Max and Minnie recorded the temperature on the first day of each month for a whole year.

Write the temperature shown on the thermometer for each month.

Don't forget to write °C.

January

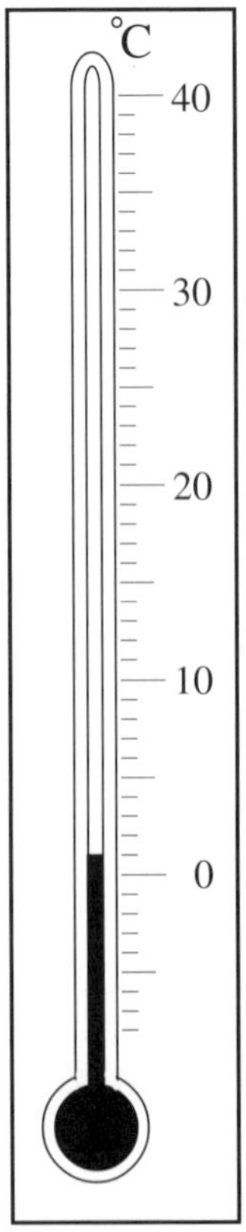


Cold.

°C

February

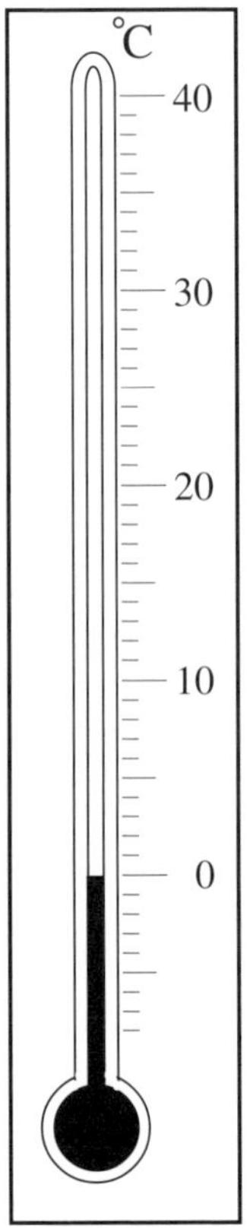


Very cold.

March

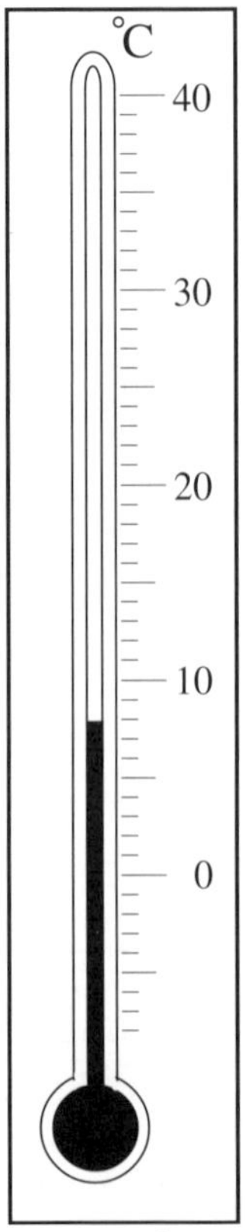


Cool.

# Removable Answer Section

Page 2 a 26 b 38 c 19 d 48 e 49 f 64

g 39 h 47 i 87 j 89 k 78 l 98

Page 3 a 61 b 83 c 61 d 89 e 84 f 68 g 76 h 95

Mental Speed: 1 11 2 14 3 15 4 11 5 14 6 12 7 13 8 14 9 17 10 13

11 13 12 12 13 18 14 15 15 13 16 12 17 11 18 16 19 12 20 10

Page 4 a 45 b 57 c 60 d 62 e 63 f 85 g 100

Page 5 a 382 b 588 c 898 d 980 e 797 f 395 g 889 h 426 i 957

Mental Speed: 1 19 2 19 3 25 4 19 5 28 6 15 7 28 8 28 9 16 10 18

11 20 12 22 13 22 14 24 15 26 16 24 17 24 18 30 19 31 20 30

Page 6 a 11 b 13 c 12 d 42 e 52 f 22 g 24 h 24 i 11 j 42 k 63 l 32 m 13 n 36 o 36 p 54 q 11 r 75

Page 7 a 28 b 26 c 15 d 43 e 28 f 34 g 58 h 27

Mental Speed: 1 4 2 4 3 5 4 6 5 9 6 3 7 8 8 5 9 7 10 5

11 9 12 5 13 5 14 2 15 7 16 4 17 5 18 4 19 2 20 8

Page 8 a 27 b 39 c 44 d 33 e 26 f 65 g 36

Page 9 a 239 b 424 c 709 d 815 e 825 f 261 g 625 h 904 i 245

Mental Speed: 1 16 2 26 3 11 4 12 5 18 6 13 7 9 8 12 9 14 10 16

11 26 12 25 13 23 14 13 15 32 16 38 17 34 18 31 19 45 20 49

Page 10 a odd b odd c even d odd e even f even g even h odd i even j even k odd l odd

Page 11

a 23
b 1216
c 340
d 999
e 2702
f 682

three hundred and forty
six hundred and eighty-two
two thousand, seven hundred and two
twenty-three
nine hundred and ninety-nine
one thousand, two hundred and sixteen

g 57 100 318 725 796
h 48 276 616 3497 9000
i 4,610
j 554
k 6,281
l 1,001

Mental Speed: 1 14 2 8 3 20 4 14 5 17 6 11 7 18 8 12 9 16 10 19
11 15 12 13 13 20 14 20 15 20 16 12 17 17 18 7 19 8 20 9

Page 13 a 7cm 2mm b 6cm c 10cm 5mm d 1cm 6mm e 10cm

f 3cm g 8cm 1mm h 6cm 5mm i 9cm

Mental Speed: 1 30 2 70 3 60 4 90 5 70 6 70 7 90 8 90 9 80 10 90
11 80 12 80 13 50 14 100 15 70 16 100 17 28 18 63 19 95 20 94

Page 14

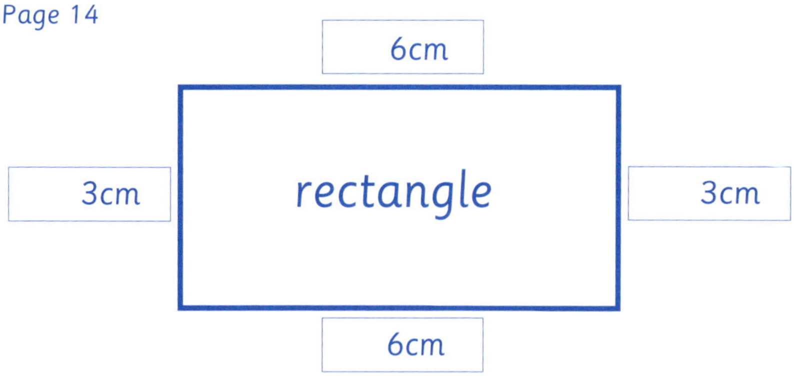


The perimeter of the rectangle is 18cm

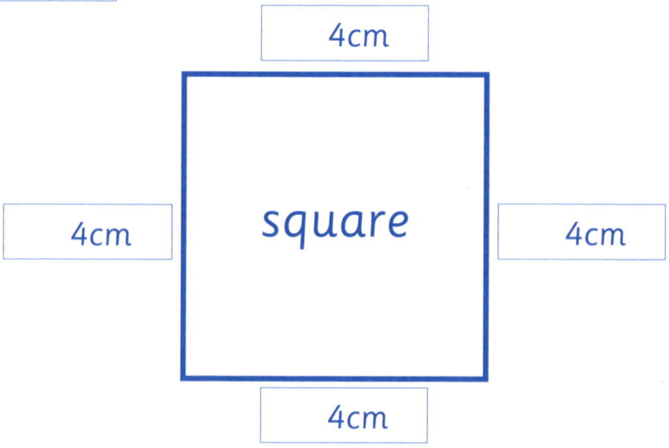


The perimeter of the square is 16cm

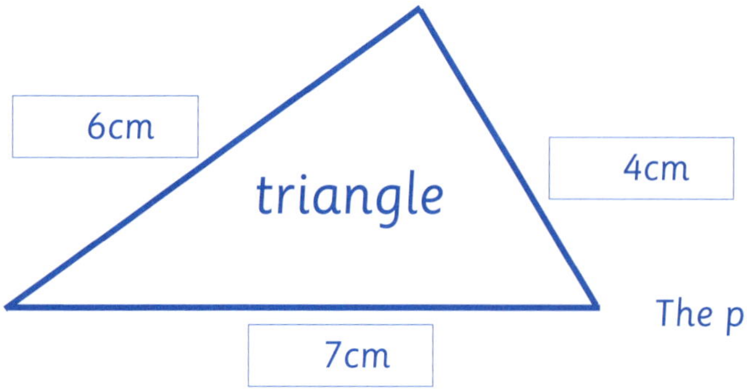


The perimeter of the triangle is 17cm

Page 15
square has 4 sides and 4 vertices
rectangle has 4 sides and 4 vertices
hexagon has 6 sides and 6 vertices
pentagon has 5 sides and 5 vertices
heptagon has 7 sides and 7 vertices
octogon has 8 sides and 8 vertices

Mental Speed:

1 10 2 30 3 0 4 50 5 50 6 10 7 30 8 70 9 70 10 40

11 40 12 60 13 40 14 30 15 40 16 60 17 59 18 37 19 55 20 76

Page 16

| | | | | |
|---|---|---|---|---|
| 2 x 2 = 4 | 3 x 3 = 9 | 2 x 4 = 8 | 1 x 5 = 5 | 2 x 6 = 12 |
| 6 x 2 = 12 | 5 x 3 = 15 | 5 x 4 = 20 | 4 x 5 = 20 | 4 x 6 = 24 |
| 8 x 2 = 16 | 8 x 3 = 24 | 7 x 4 = 28 | 5 x 5 = 25 | 6 x 6 = 36 |
| 10 x 2 = 20 | 10 x 3 = 30 | 9 x 4 = 36 | 7 x 5 = 35 | 8 x 6 = 48 |
| | | | 8 x 5 = 40 | 10 x 6 = 60 |
| | | | 10 x 5 = 50 | |

Page 17

| | | | |
|---|---|---|---|
| 1 x 7 = 7 | 2 x 8 = 16 | 1 x 9 = 9 | 2 x 10 = 20 |
| 3 x 7 = 21 | 4 x 8 = 32 | 4 x 9 = 36 | 4 x 10 = 40 |
| 5 x 7 = 35 | 6 x 8 = 48 | 5 x 9 = 45 | 6 x 10 = 60 |
| 7 x 7 = 49 | 8 x 8 = 64 | 7 x 9 = 63 | 8 x 10 = 80 |
| 9 x 7 = 63 | 10 x 8 = 80 | 8 x 9 = 72 | |
| | | 10 x 9 = 90 | |

Mental Speed: 1 100 2 42 3 20 4 27 5 32 6 42 7 24 8 45 9 56 10 60

11 20 12 63 13 16 14 24 15 72 16 18 17 64 18 54 19 14 20 40

Page 18 a 28 b 69 c 48 d 62 e 48 f 86

Page 19 a 72 b 45 c 54 d 85 e 70 f 68 g 96 h 92

Mental Speed: 1 30 2 35 3 36 4 72 5 28 6 63 7 48 8 15 9 14 10 90

11 32 12 49 13 40 14 32 15 36 16 30 17 56 18 45 19 8 20 70

Page 20 January 1 °C February 0 °C March 8 °C

Page 21 April 14 °C May 17 °C June 21 °C July 25 °C August 28 °C
September 20 °C October 15 °C November 8 °C December 5 °C

Page 22 Answers can be found by comparing the chart to Max's table.

Page 23 a 9 b 10 c 7 d 29 e 35

Mental Speed: 1 22 2 48 3 56 4 95 5 29 6 77 7 69 8 31 9 32 10 76

11 83 12 37 13 59 14 94 15 94 16 62 17 69 18 73 19 48 20 99

Page 24 a 9 b 6 c 4 d 4 e 6 f 4 g 6 h 7 i 4 j 7 k 10 l 8 m 8 n 7

Page 25 a 7 r 1 b 4 c 5 r 1 d 4 r 3 e 4 r 2 f 9 r 1 g 5 h 5 r 5 i 6 r 4 j 4 r 4

Mental Speed: 1 3 2 6 3 4 4 3 5 9 6 7 7 7 8 7 9 2 10 3

11 4 12 5 13 4 14 8 15 8 16 8 17 6 18 7 19 9 20 5

Page 26 a 564 b 390 c 369 d 980 e 893 f 876 g 918 h 637 i 900 j 918 k 926 l 871 m 645 n 665

o 427 p 238 q 252 r 548 s 338 t 374 u 387 v 814 w 657

Page 27 a 88 b 60 c 96 d 76 e 96 f 65 g 72 h 78 i 5r2 j 11 k 7r1 l 5r2 m 7r3 n 8 o 7 p 7r1 q 4r1 r 8

Mental Speed: 1 32 2 4 3 8 4 56 5 7 6 8 7 45 8 5 9 9 10 21

11 36 12 81 13 25 14 64 15 8 16 6 17 9 18 3 19 5 20 4

Page 28 a 61 cm b 92p c 8p d 2 e 6 f 2p g 76 h 806 i 28

Page 29 a 2, 4, 6, 8, 10, 12, 14 b 7, 8, 9, 10, 11, 12, 13 c 21, 20, 19, 18, 17, 16, 15

d 1, 1, 2, 2, 3, 3, 4 e 5, 10, 15, 20, 25, 30, 35 f 1, 3, 2, 4, 3, 5, 4

g 100, 200, 300, 400, 500, 600, 700 h 50, 100, 150, 200, 250, 300, 350

Mental Speed: 1 100 2 50 3 200 4 700 5 750 6 50 7 75 8 100 9 75 10 25

11 40 12 100 13 60 14 80 15 80 16 20 17 40 18 60 19 80 20 100

Page 30 b half past nine, 9:30 d half past eleven, 11:30 e a quarter past ten, 10:15
f a quarter to eight, 7:45 g a quarter past nine, 9:15 h eight o'clock, 8:00
i a quarter to six, 5:45

Page 31 a 30 minutes b 15 minutes c 120 minutes

Page 32 b five minutes to seven c ten minutes past four, 4:10 d 1:20 e twenty minutes to eight, 7:40
f twenty-five minutes past twelve, 12:25

Page 33 a 30 b 20 c 20 d 15 e 25 f 10 g

10:50

h 30 minutes

Mental Speed: 1 14 2 16 3 8 4 12 5 8 6 18 7 15 8 14 9 10 10 17

11 8 12 8 13 8 14 5 15 7 16 9 17 5 18 9 19 5 20 12

Page 34 a $\frac{1}{2}$ b $\frac{3}{4}$ c $\frac{1}{2}$ d $\frac{1}{4}$ e half f half g three quarters h quarter i half j half

Page 35 a four stars should be coloured b 9 c 6 d 8 e 6 f 4 g 7

Mental Speed: 1 2 2 8 3 4 4 3 5 9 6 1 7 7 8 10 9 5 10 2

11 1 12 8 13 6 14 7 15 20 16 50 17 30 18 3 19 6 20 10

Page 37 a 4 b 4 c 300 grams d 50 grams e 75 grams f

2:40

Mental Speed: 1 15 2 35 3 10 4 30 5 45 6 20 7 40 8 25 9 50 10 30

11 50 12 90 13 60 14 50 15 75 16 100 17 90 18 40 19 70 20 90

Page 38 a East b West c West

Page 39 a South-West b South

Mental Speed: 1 4 2 7 3 6 4 5 5 6 6 9 7 3 8 9 9 7 10 9

11 8 12 7 13 10 14 5 15 9 16 5 17 4 18 4 19 8 20 4

Page 40 a 736 b 804 c 398 d 800 e 700 f 513 g 461 h 337 i 728 j 723

k 75 l 76 m 80 n 85 o 96 p 6 q 6r3 r 7 s 7r1 t 6

April

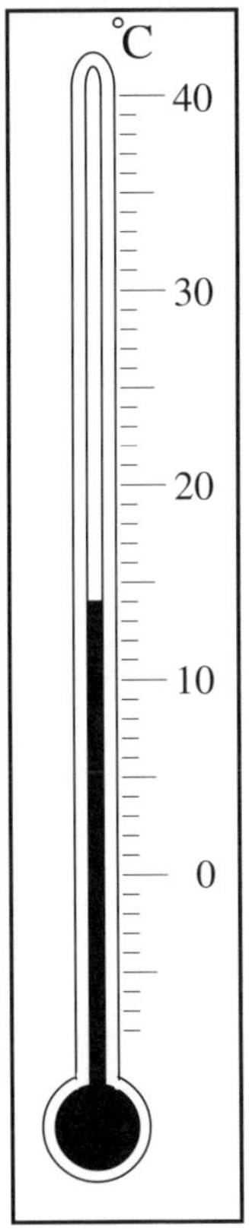


Milder.

May

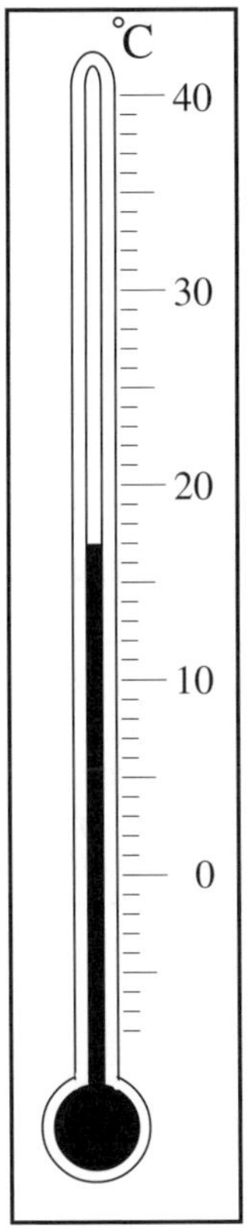


Warmer.

June

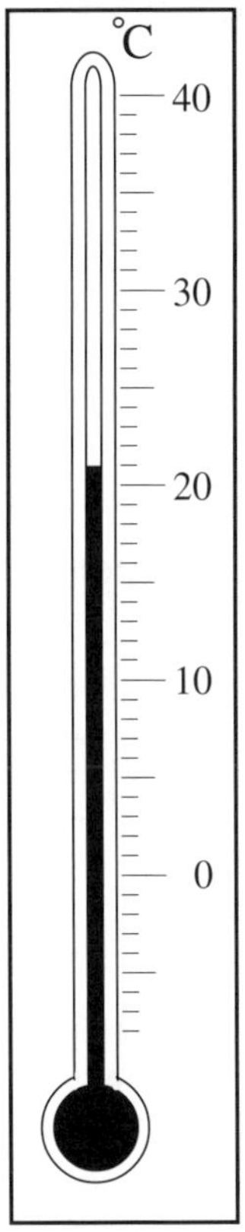


Warm.

July

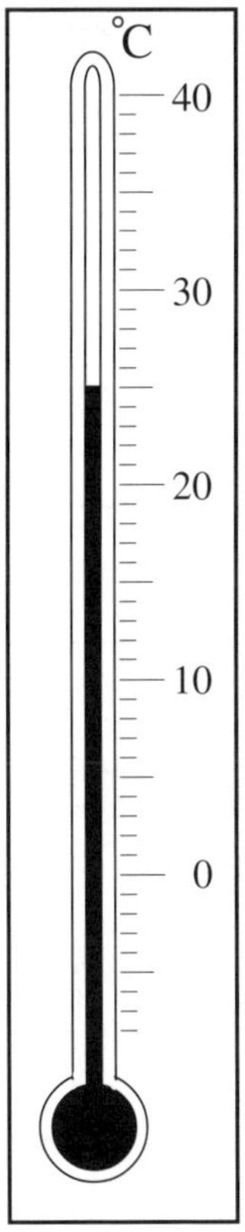


Hot.

August

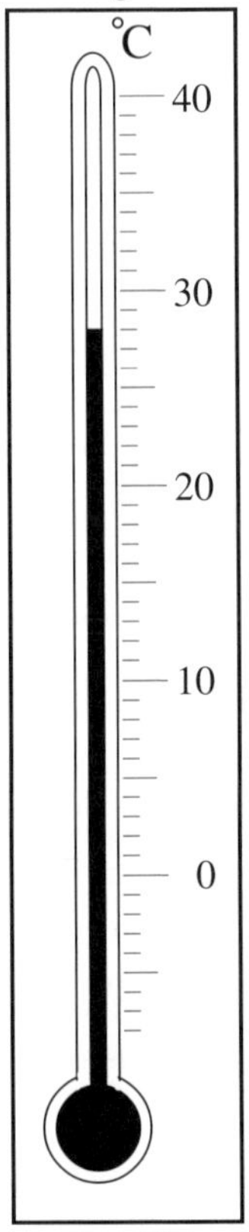


Very hot.

September

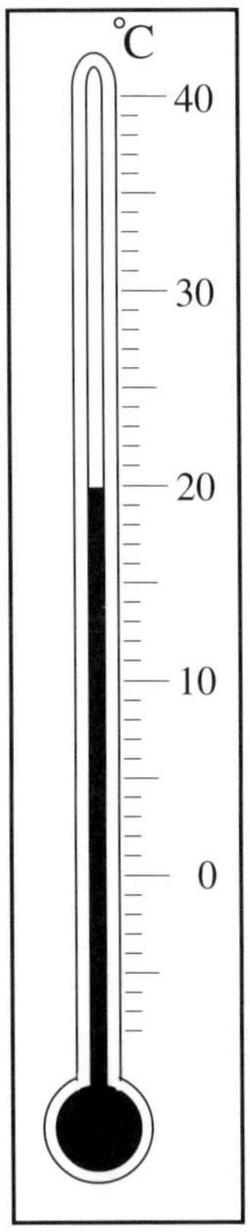


Warm.

October

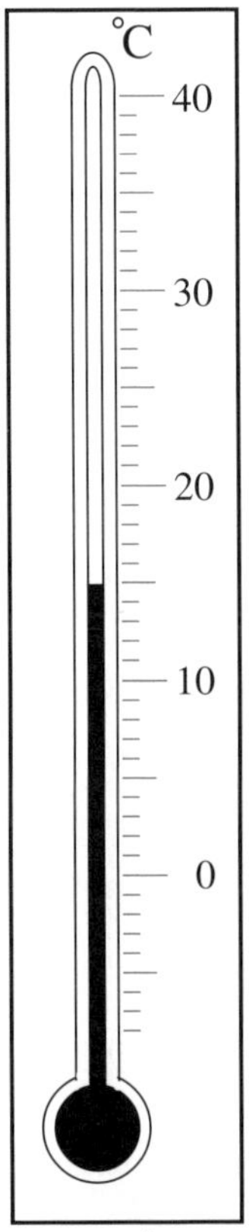


Cooler.

November

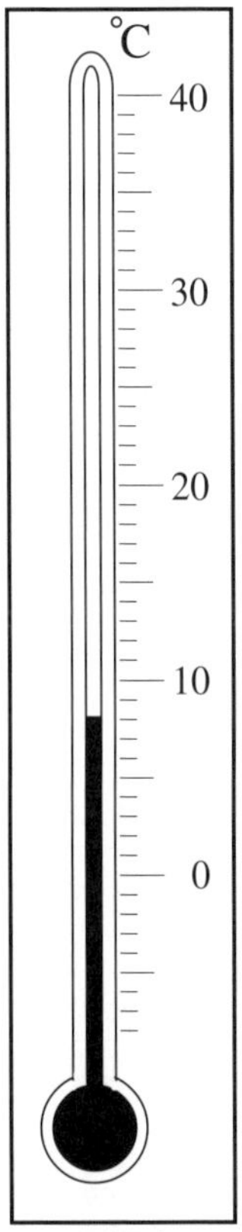


Cool.

December

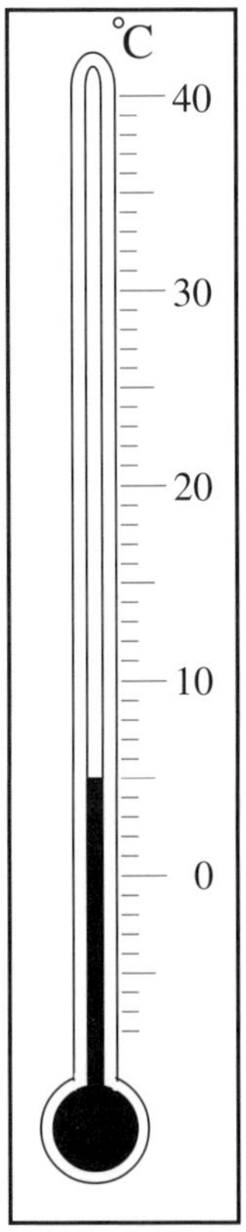


Cold.

# Handling Data

| My Table of Temperatures Over One Year by Max | | | | | | | | | | | | |
|---|---|---|---|---|---|---|---|---|---|---|---|---|
| Month | Jan | Feb | Mar | Apr | May | Jun | Jul | Aug | Sep | Oct | Nov | Dec |
| Temperature in °C | 1 | 0 | 8 | 14 | 17 | 21 | 25 | 28 | 20 | 15 | 8 | 5 |

Minnie's bar chart has been started. Fill in the rest of the chart.

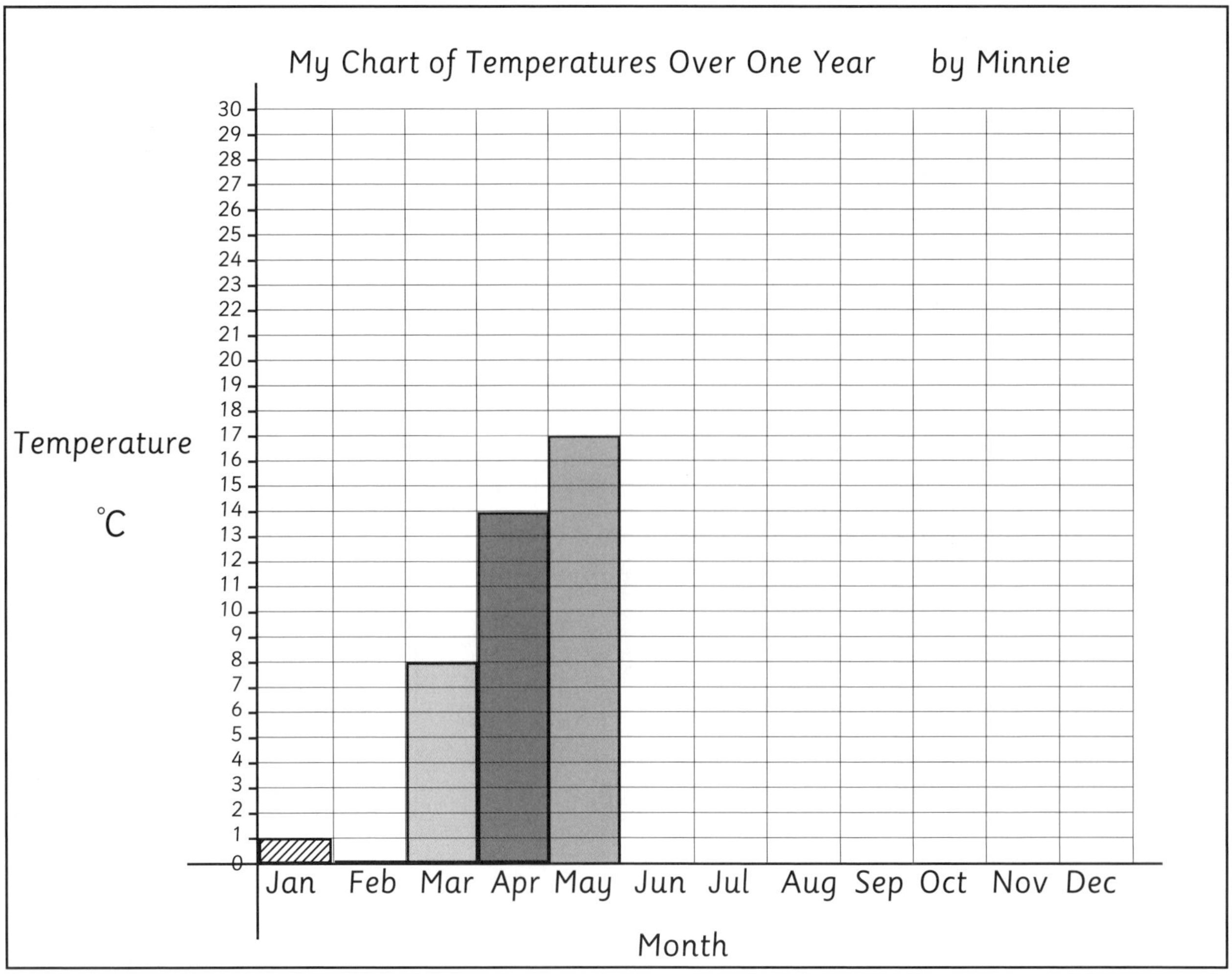

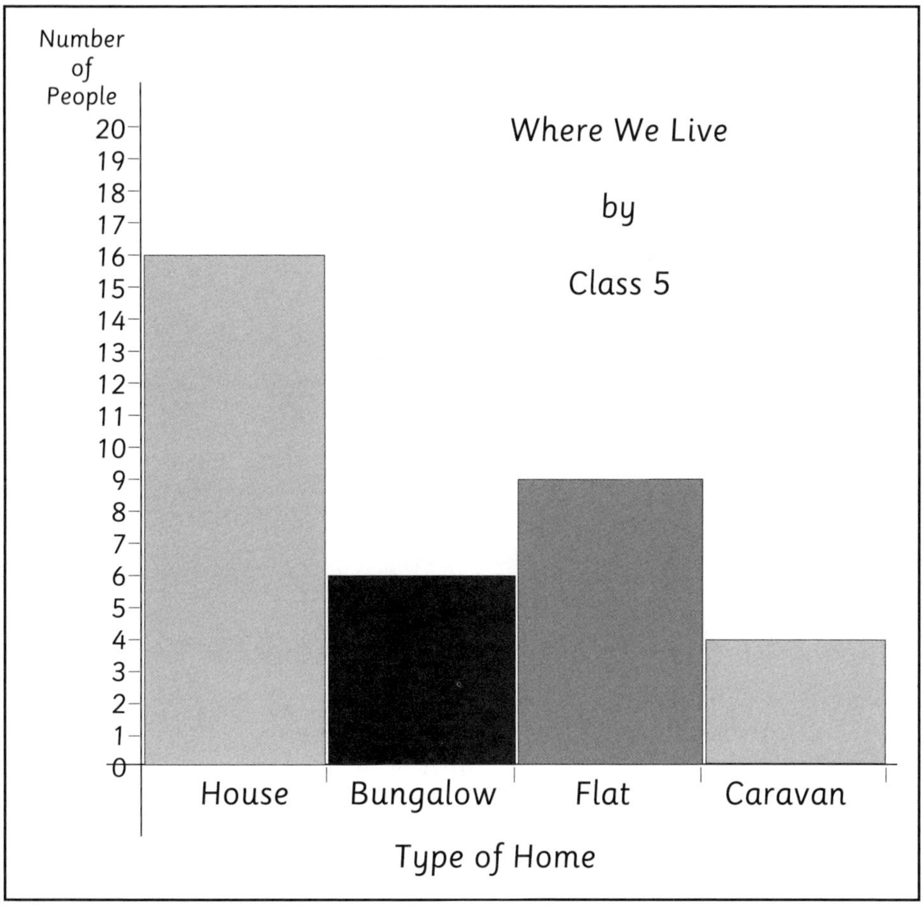


Use the chart to find the answers to these questions:

| | |
|---|---|
| (a) How many people live in a flat? | |
| (b) How many more people live in a house than in a bungalow? | |
| (c) How many fewer people live in a flat than in a house? | |
| (d) How many people do not live in a bungalow? | |
| (e) How many people are there in Class 5 altogether? | |

## Mental Speed

How quickly can you answer these questions?
Time yourself and record your score.

1) 12 + 10 =
2) 38 + 10 =
3) 46 + 10 =
4) 85 + 10 =
5) 10 + 19 =
6) 10 + 67 =
7) 10 + 59 =
8) 21 + 10 =
9) 12 + 20 =
10) 56 + 20 =
11) 63 + 20 =
12) 20 + 17 =
13) 20 + 39 =
14) 20 + 74 =
15) 64 + 30 =
16) 32 + 30 =
17) 39 + 30 =
18) 30 + 43 =
19) 30 + 18 =
20) 30 + 69 =

Time taken:

☐ minutes and

☐ seconds.

# Division

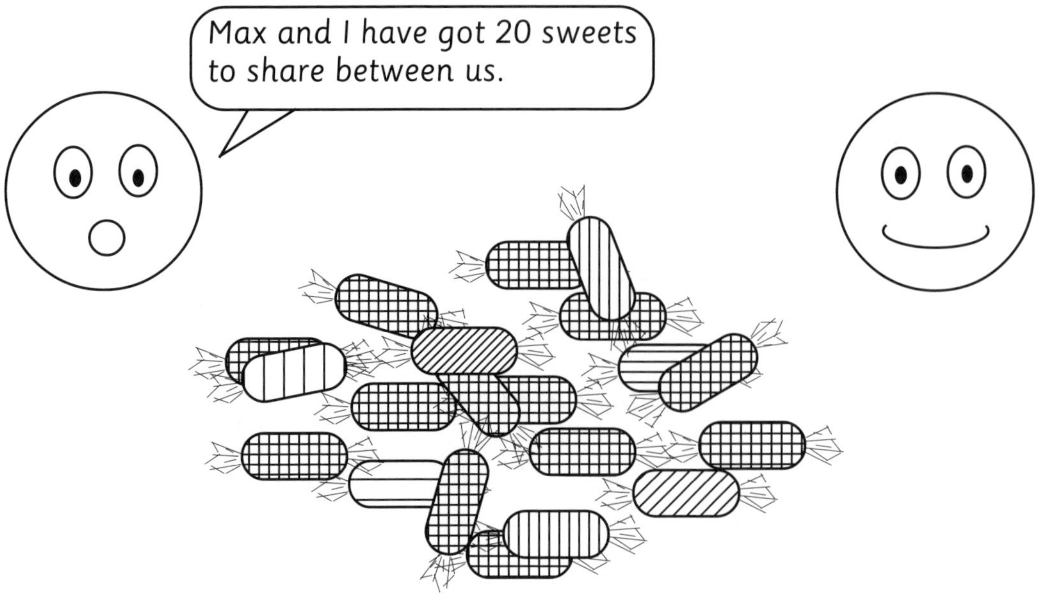


They can have ten sweets each because twenty shared between two is ten.

We can write this in two ways: $20 \div 2 = 10$ or $\begin{array}{r} 10 \\ 2\overline{)20} \end{array}$

You can use your multiplication tables to help you with division:

Sixteen divided by two is eight because eight twos are sixteen and two eights are sixteen.

$8 \times 2 = 16$

$2 \times 8 = 16$

$16 \div 2 = 8$ or $\begin{array}{r} 8 \\ 2\overline{)16} \end{array}$

Use your multiplication tables to help you with these divisions:

| | | | |
|---|---|---|---|
| (a) $18 \div 2 =$ | (b) $12 \div 2 =$ | (c) $16 \div 4 =$ | (d) $24 \div 6 =$ |
| (e) $18 \div 3 =$ | (f) $32 \div 8 =$ | (g) $42 \div 7 =$ | (h) $63 \div 9 =$ |

| | | | | | |
|---|---|---|---|---|---|
| (i) $9\overline{)36}$ | (j) $5\overline{)35}$ | (k) $4\overline{)40}$ | (l) $9\overline{)72}$ | (m) $8\overline{)64}$ | (n) $6\overline{)42}$ |

We say that 21 divided by 2 is 10 remainder 1.

$21 \div 2 = 10 \text{ r } 1$

$$\begin{array}{r} 10 \text{ r } 1 \\ 2\overline{)21} \end{array}$$

Try to work out these divisions.
Some of them will have remainders.

(a) $15 \div 2 =$

(b) $12 \div 3 =$

(c) $16 \div 3 =$

(d) $19 \div 4 =$

(e) $26 \div 6 =$

(f) $37 \div 4 =$

(g) $8\overline{)40}$

(h) $7\overline{)40}$

(i) $6\overline{)40}$

(j) $9\overline{)40}$

## Mental Speed

How quickly can you answer these questions?
Time yourself and record your score.

1) $12 \div 4 =$
2) $42 \div 7 =$
3) $36 \div 9 =$
4) $24 \div 8 =$
5) $18 \div 2 =$
6) $42 \div 6 =$
7) $63 \div 9 =$
8) $21 \div 3 =$
9) $12 \div 6 =$
10) $27 \div 9 =$
11) $32 \div 8 =$
12) $20 \div 4 =$
13) $20 \div 5 =$
14) $48 \div 6 =$
15) $64 \div 8 =$
16) $32 \div 4 =$
17) $36 \div 6 =$
18) $49 \div 7 =$
19) $81 \div 9 =$
20) $30 \div 6 =$

Time taken:

☐ minutes and

☐ seconds.

# Addition and Subtraction Practice Page

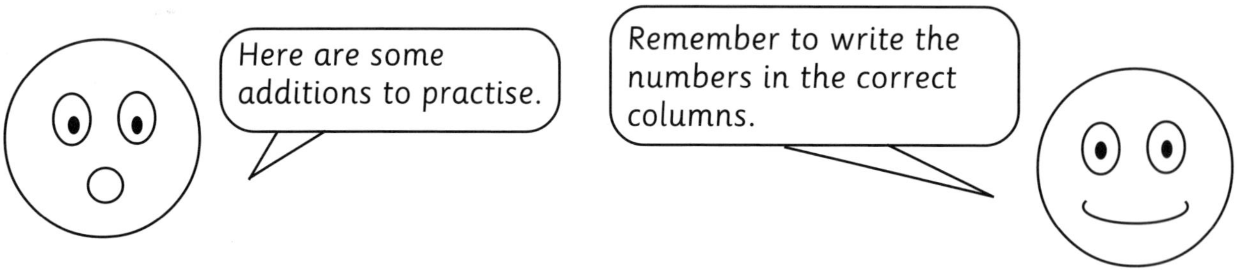


| | | | | |
|---|---|---|---|---|
| (a) 426 + 138 | (b) 307 + 83 | (c) 252 + 117 | (d) 945 + 35 | (e) 686 + 207 |
| (f) 564 + 312 | (g) 747 + 171 | (h) 349 + 288 | (i) 673 + 227 | (j) 849 + 69 |

(k) 650 + 276

(l) 814 + 57

(m) 398 + 247

(n) 589 + 76

Now try these subtractions:

| | | | | |
|---|---|---|---|---|
| (o) 569 - 142 | (p) 473 - 235 | (q) 824 - 572 | (r) 633 - 85 | (s) 704 - 366 |

(t) 650 - 276

(u) 600 - 213

(v) 983 - 169

(w) 744 - 87

# Multiplication and Division Practice Page

Do you remember how to work out these multiplications? You might need to look back at page 19.

| | | | |
|---|---|---|---|
| (a) 44 x 2 | (b) 15 x 4 | (c) 32 x 3 | (d) 38 x 2 |
| (e) 16 x 6 | (f) 13 x 5 | (g) 18 x 4 | (h) 26 x 3 |

These divisions are like the ones on page 25.

| | |
|---|---|
| (i) 17 ÷ 3 = | (j) 22 ÷ 2 = |
| (k) 22 ÷ 3 = | (l) 22 ÷ 4 = |
| (m) 38 ÷ 5 = | (n) 48 ÷ 6 = |

| | | | |
|---|---|---|---|
| (o) 7)49 | (p) 9)64 | (q) 8)33 | (r) 5)40 |

## Mental Speed

How quickly can you answer these questions?
Time yourself and record your score.

1) 8 x 4 =
2) 32 ÷ 8 =
3) 32 ÷ 4 =
4) 7 x 8 =
5) 56 ÷ 8 =
6) 56 ÷ 7 =
7) 5 x 9 =
8) 45 ÷ 9 =
9) 45 ÷ 5 =
10) 7 x 3 =
11) 6 x 6 =
12) 9 x 9 =
13) 5 x 5 =
14) 8 x 8 =
15) 64 ÷ 8 =
16) 36 ÷ 6 =
17) 81 ÷ 9 =
18) 21 ÷ 7 =
19) 25 ÷ 5 =
20) 16 ÷ 4 =

Time taken:

☐ minutes and

☐ seconds.

# Number Problems

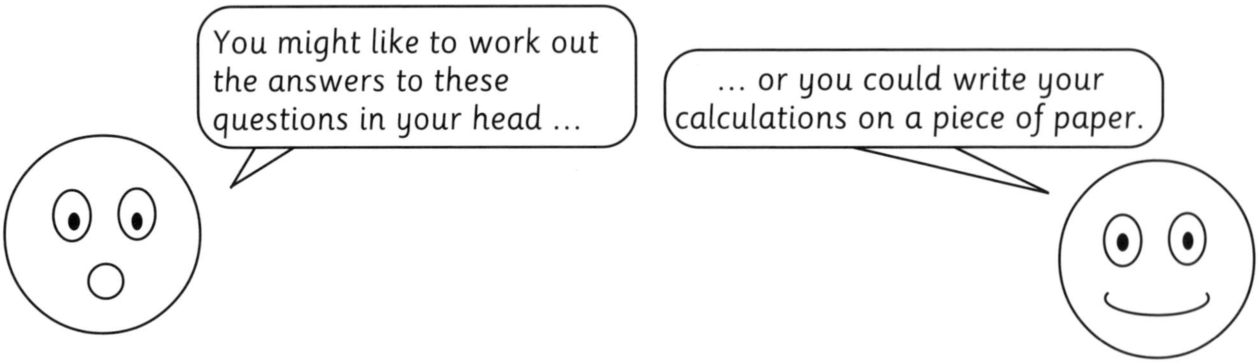


(a) A piece of wood is 98 cm long.
If Max cuts off 37 cm, how much is left?

(b) Ice lollies cost 23p each.
How much should I pay for 4 of these lollies?

(c) How much change will I get from £1 when I buy these four ice lollies?

(d) At a party there are 18 cakes on a plate and there are 9 children.
If the cakes are shared out fairly between them, how many cakes does each child have?

(e) Minnie has got 50p and wants to buy some stickers which are 8p each.
How many stickers can Minnie afford to buy?

(f) How much money will Minnie have left out of the 50p ?

(g) At a furniture factory they have made 19 table-tops.
How many legs do they need to make for these tables?

(h) In a big school there are 417 boys and 389 girls.
How many children are there in that school?

(i) How many more boys are there than girls?

# Number Sequences

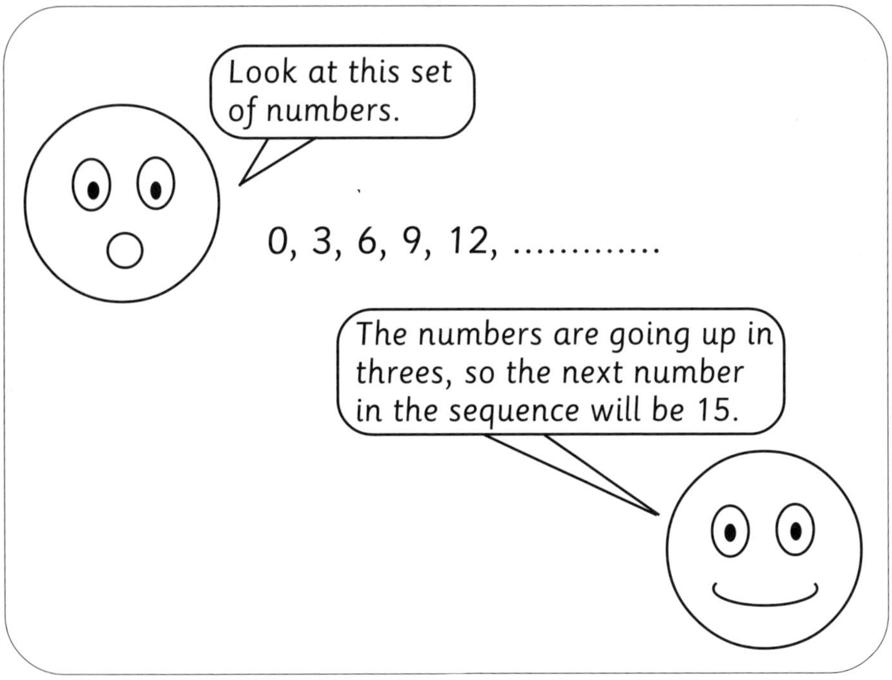


Try to fill the gaps in these sequences:

| | | | | | | | |
|---|---|---|---|---|---|---|---|
| (a) | 2 | 4 | 6 | 8 | 10 | | |
| (b) | 7 | 8 | 9 | 10 | | | 13 |
| (c) | 21 | 20 | 19 | 18 | 17 | | |
| (d) | 1 | 1 | 2 | 2 | 3 | | |
| (e) | 5 | 10 | 15 | 20 | | | 35 |
| (f) | 1 | 3 | 2 | 4 | 3 | 5 | |
| (g) | 100 | 200 | 300 | | 500 | | 700 |
| (h) | 50 | 100 | 150 | 200 | 250 | | |

## Mental Speed

How quickly can you answer these questions?
Time yourself and record your score.

1) 50 + 50 =

2) 100 - 50 =

3) 250 - 50 =

4) 650 + 50 =

5) 800 - 50 =

6) 25 + 25 =

7) 50 + 25 =

8) 75 + 25 =

9) 100 - 25 =

10) 100 - 75 =

11) 20 + 20 =

12) 80 + 20 =

13) 40 + 20 =

14) 60 + 20 =

15) 100 - 20 =

16) 1 x 20 =

17) 2 x 20 =

18) 3 x 20 =

19) 4 x 20 =

20) 5 x 20 =

Time taken:

☐ minutes and

☐ seconds.

# Time

half past four

4:30

For each clock, write the time in two ways:

(a)

a quarter past seven

7:15

(b)

(c)

a quarter to two

1:45

(d)

(e)

(f)

(g)

(h)

(i)

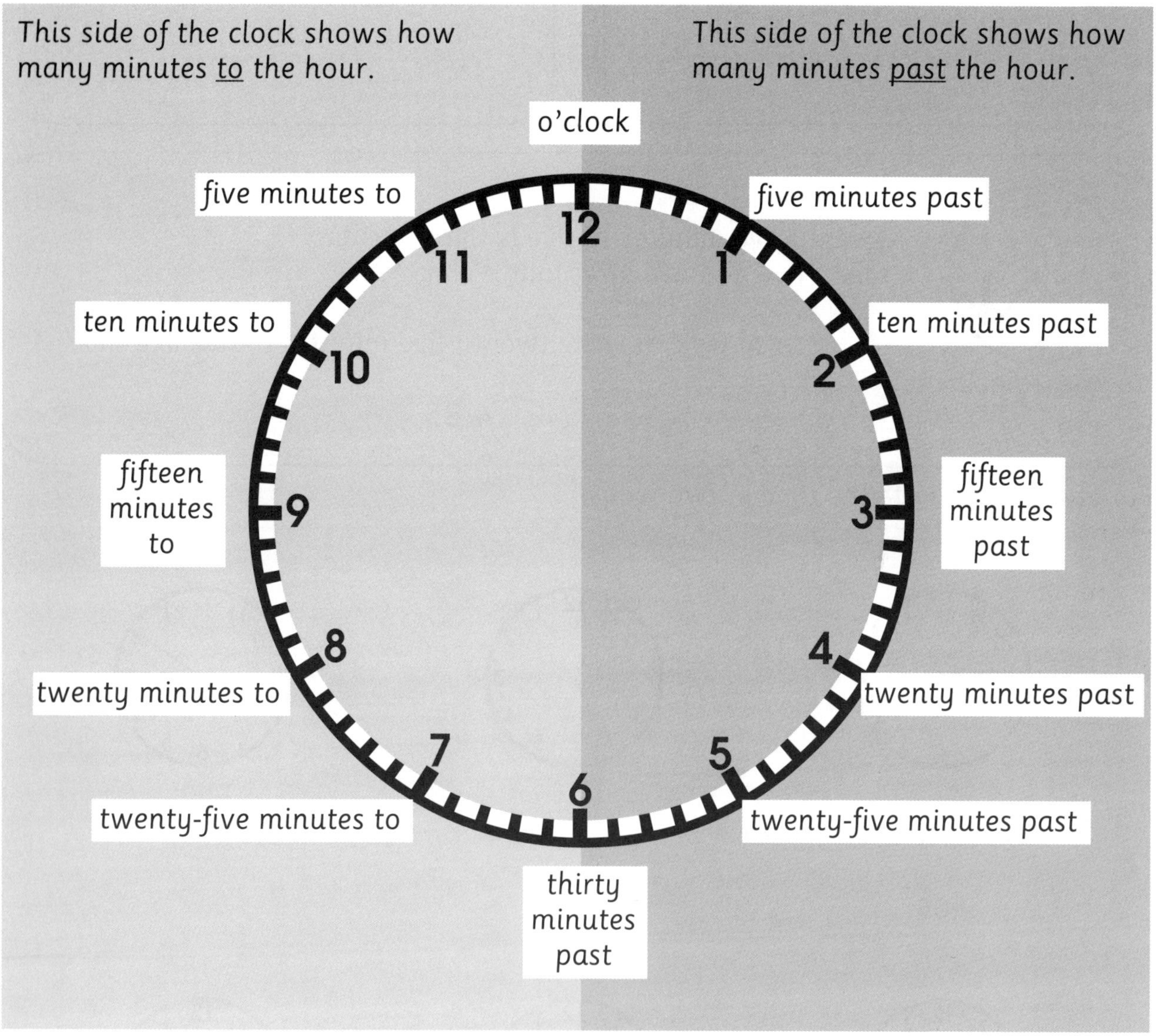


| | | |
|---|---|---|
| a | How many minutes are there in half an hour? | minutes |
| b | How many minutes are there in a quarter of an hour? | |
| c | How many minutes are there in two hours? | |

# More Time

The time shown on this clock is ten past six.

ten past six

6:10

This clock shows twenty-five minutes to five.

twenty-five to five

twenty-five to five

Twenty-five minutes to five is the same as thirty-five minutes after four o'clock ....

..... so we can write twenty-five minutes to five like this:

4:35

For each clock, write the time in two ways:

(a)

five minutes past nine

9:05

(b)

6:55

(c)

(d)

twenty minutes past one

(e)

(f)

a) 1 hour = 30 minutes + ☐ minutes

b) 1 hour = 40 minutes + ☐ minutes

c) $\frac{1}{2}$ hour = 10 minutes + ☐ minutes

d) $\frac{1}{2}$ hour = 15 minutes + ☐ minutes

e) $\frac{1}{2}$ hour = 5 minutes + ☐ minutes

f) $\frac{1}{4}$ hour = 5 minutes + ☐ minutes

g) Breaktime starts at 10:30 and lasts for 20 minutes.

Draw the hands on the clock to show the end of breaktime. Write the time underneath.

10:30

h) A television programme starts at five minutes to five and finishes at twenty past five. How long is this programme?

## Mental Speed

How quickly can you answer these questions?
Time yourself and record your score.

1) 6 + 8 =

2) 7 + 9 =

3) 2 + 6 =

4) 4 + 8 =

5) 5 + 3 =

6) 9 + 9 =

7) 8 + 7 =

8) 7 + 7 =

9) 2 + 8 =

10) 8 + 9 =

11) 14 - 6 =

12) 17 - 9 =

13) 13 - 5 =

14) 12 - 7 =

15) 15 - 8 =

16) 16 - 7 =

17) 14 - 9 =

18) 18 - 9 =

19) 13 - 8 =

20) 16 - 4 =

Time taken:

☐ minutes and

☐ seconds.

# Fractions

How much of each shape is shaded?

Write the correct fraction in the box under each picture.

Write: $\frac{1}{4}$ or $\frac{1}{2}$ or $\frac{3}{4}$

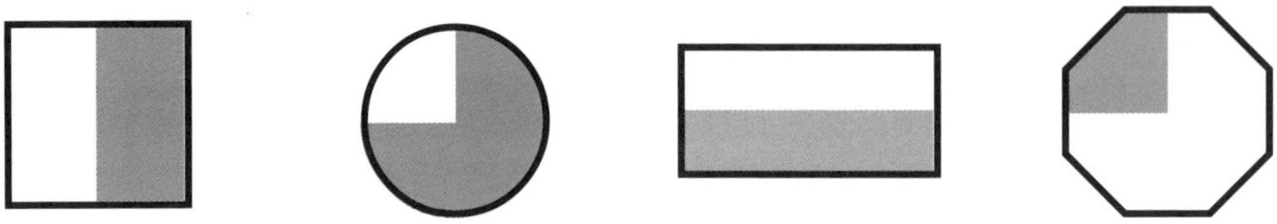

(a) (b) (c) (d)

This picture shows that a half is the same amount as two quarters.

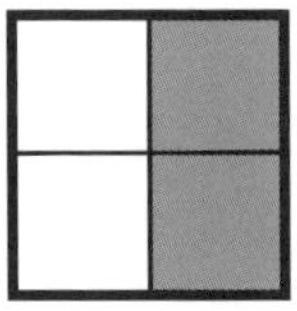

two quarters = one half

$\frac{2}{4} = \frac{1}{2}$

So in this picture we can still say that half the square is shaded.

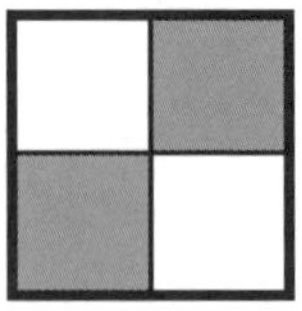

two quarters = one half

$\frac{2}{4} = \frac{1}{2}$

For each shape below write in words how much is shaded and how much is not shaded.

Write: quarter or half or three-quarters

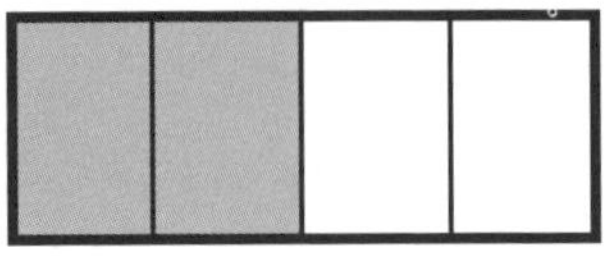

(e) shaded:

(f) not shaded:

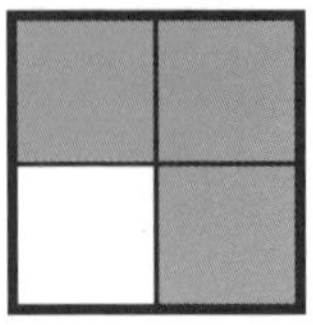

(g) shaded:

(h) not shaded:

(i) shaded:

(j) not shaded:

There are six circles. Three of them are black.

Half of the circles are black.

(a) Colour half of the stars red.

Sometimes we need to find a fraction of a number.

$\frac{1}{2}$ of 10 = 5

$\frac{1}{4}$ of 12 = 3

You can use the multiplication tables on pages 16 and 17 to help you with these questions:

| | | | |
|---|---|---|---|
| (b) | $\frac{1}{2}$ of 18 = | (c) | $\frac{1}{4}$ of 24 = |
| (d) | $\frac{1}{4}$ of 32 = | (e) | $\frac{1}{2}$ of 12 = |
| (f) | $\frac{1}{4}$ of 16 = | (g) | $\frac{1}{4}$ of 28 = |

## Mental Speed

How quickly can you answer these questions?
Time yourself and record your score.

1) $\frac{1}{4}$ of 8 =

2) $\frac{1}{2}$ of 16 =

3) $\frac{1}{4}$ of 16 =

4) $\frac{1}{4}$ of 12 =

5) $\frac{1}{4}$ of 36 =

6) $\frac{1}{4}$ of 4 =

7) $\frac{1}{2}$ of 14 =

8) $\frac{1}{2}$ of 20 =

9) $\frac{1}{4}$ of 20 =

10) $\frac{1}{2}$ of 4 =

11) $\frac{1}{2}$ of 2 =

12) $\frac{1}{4}$ of 32 =

13) $\frac{1}{4}$ of 24 =

14) $\frac{1}{4}$ of 28 =

15) $\frac{1}{2}$ of 40 =

16) $\frac{1}{2}$ of 100 =

17) $\frac{1}{2}$ of 60 =

18) $\frac{3}{4}$ of 4 =

19) $\frac{3}{4}$ of 8 =

20) $\frac{1}{4}$ of 40 =

Time taken:

☐ minutes and

☐ seconds.

# Weighing in Grams

## *Simply super sponges*

*Ingredients:*

*2 eggs*
*100 grams of self-raising flour*
*100 grams of caster sugar*
*100 grams of butter (at room temperature)*
*1 level teaspoon of baking powder*

*Method:*

***Pre-heat oven to 170°C.***
***Place paper cake cases in a patty-tin.***
***Put all your ingredients into a mixing bowl.***
***Use an electric mixer to beat ingredients together for about 2 minutes.***
***Put a heaped teaspoonful of the mixture into each paper cake case.***
***Carefully place the patty-tin into the oven.***
***Leave for fifteen minutes or until golden brown.***
***Carefully remove from oven.***
***Leave to cool.***

*Take care when cooking. The oven is hot!*

A rounded tablespoon of sugar weighs approximately 25g.

A heaped tablespoon of flour weighs approximately 25g.

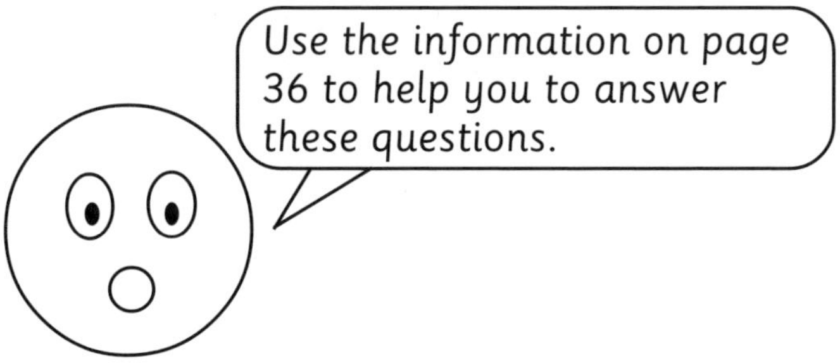


ⓐ How many rounded tablespoons of caster sugar are needed for the recipe?

ⓑ How many heaped tablespoons of flour are needed for the recipe?

ⓒ What is the total weight needed of sugar, flour and butter?

ⓓ What would be the approximate weight of two rounded tablespoons of caster sugar?

ⓔ What would be the approximate weight of three heaped tablespoons of flour?

ⓕ Max puts the cakes in the oven at twenty-five past two.

2:25

Draw the hands to show the time that the cakes should be ready, then write the time underneath.

Useful information:

A thousand grams equal one kilogram

1000 g = 1 kg

## Mental Speed

How quickly can you answer these questions?
Time yourself and record your score.

1) 3 x 5 =
2) 7 x 5 =
3) 2 x 5 =
4) 6 x 5 =
5) 9 x 5 =
6) 4 x 5 =
7) 8 x 5 =
8) 5 x 5 =
9) 10 x 5 =
10) 15 + 15 =
11) 35 + 15 =
12) 75 + 15 =
13) 15 + 45 =
14) 25 + 25 =
15) 50 + 25 =
16) 75 + 25 =
17) 65 + 25 =
18) 15 + 25 =
19) 35 + 35 =
20) 45 + 45 =

Time taken:

☐ minutes and

☐ seconds.

# Compass Directions and Right Angles

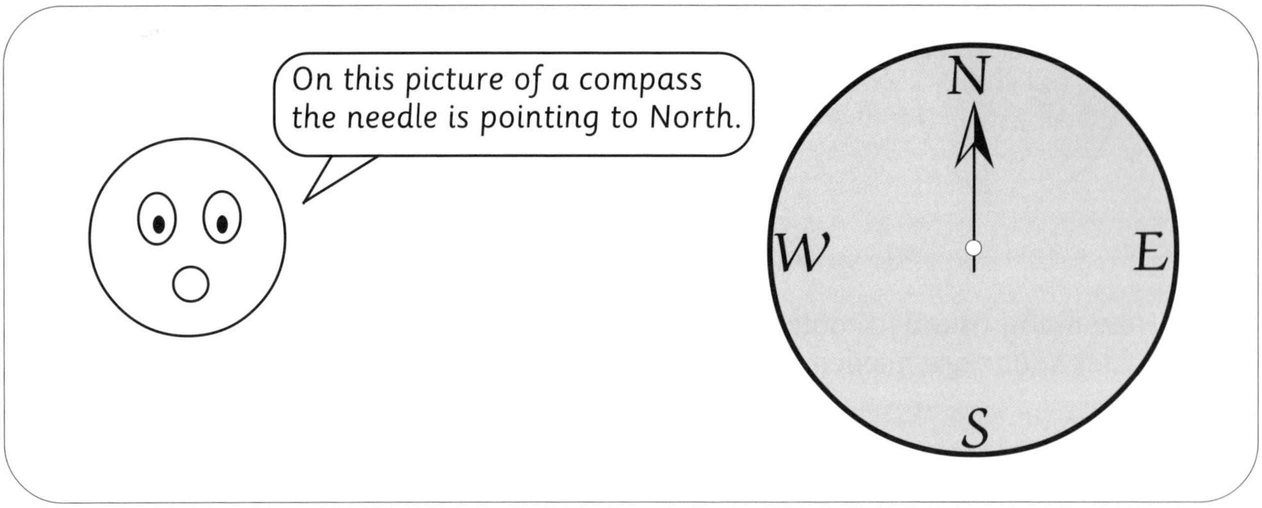


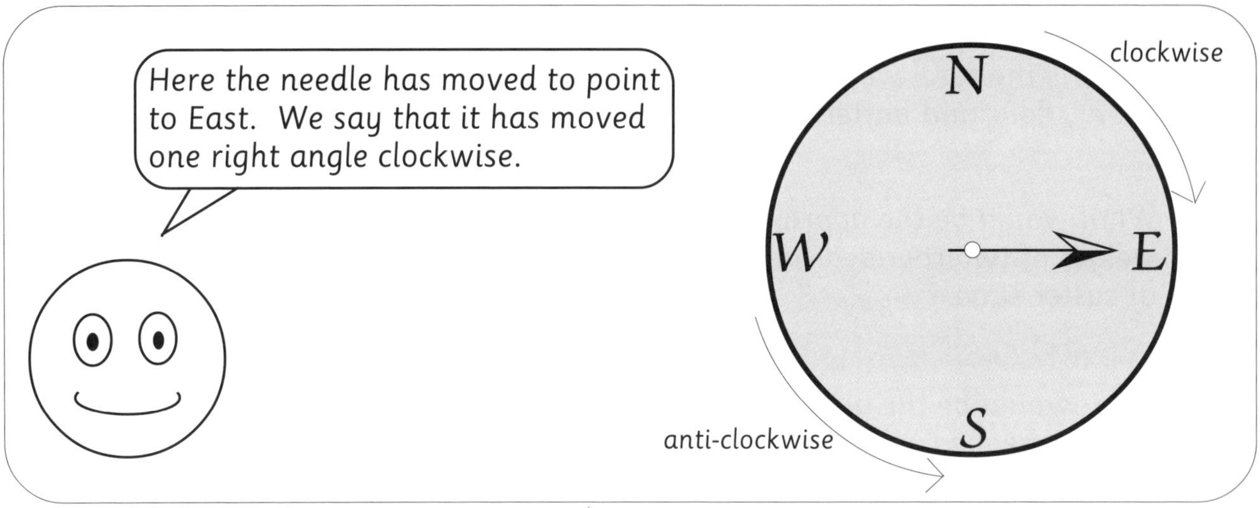


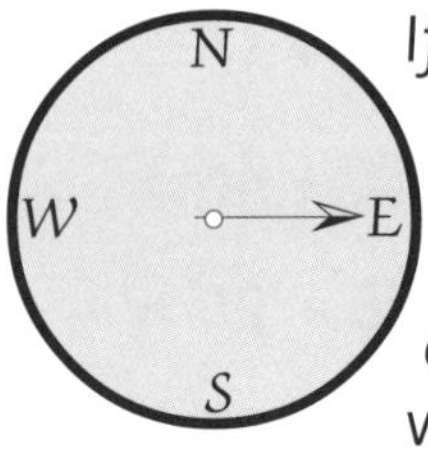


If the needle is pointing East and turns one right angle anti-clockwise it will be pointing to North again.

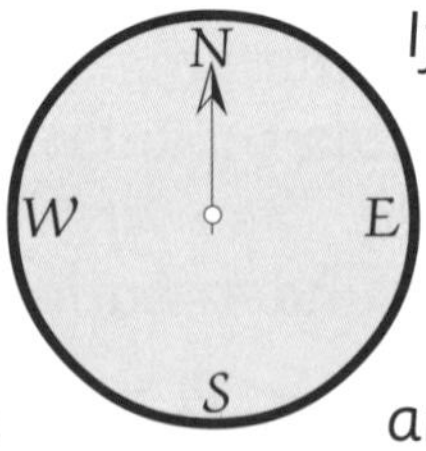


If the needle is pointing North and turns two right angles clockwise or anti-clockwise it will be pointing to South.

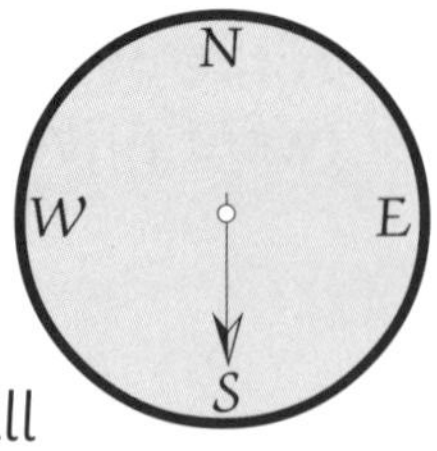


Look at the pictures of the compass to help you to answer these questions:

(a) If the compass needle is pointing West and then turns two right angles anti-clockwise, in which direction will it point?

(b) If the compass needle is pointing South and then turns one right angle clockwise, in which direction will it point?

(c) If the compass needle is pointing North and then turns one right angle anti-clockwise, in which direction will it point?

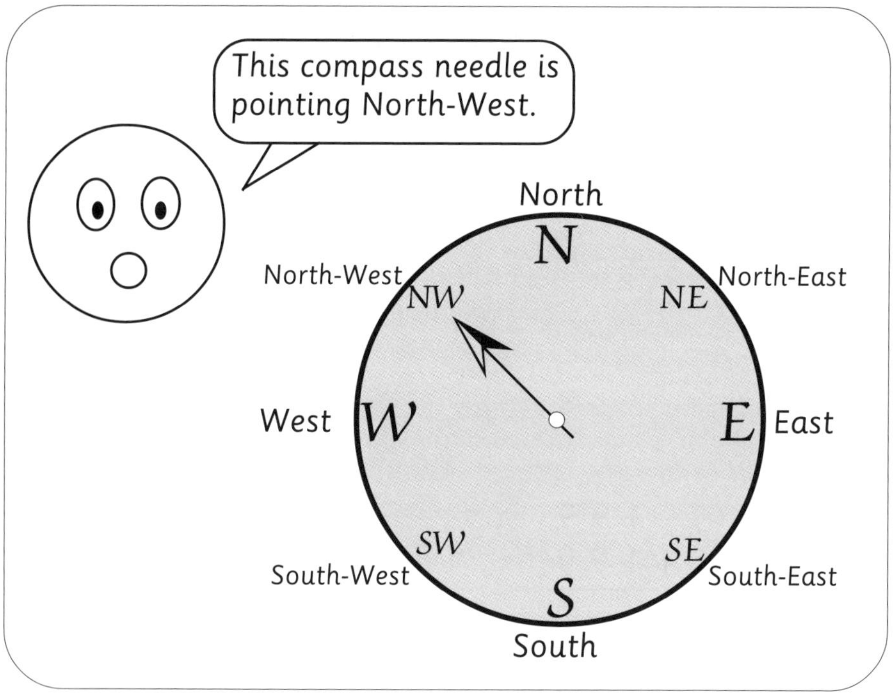


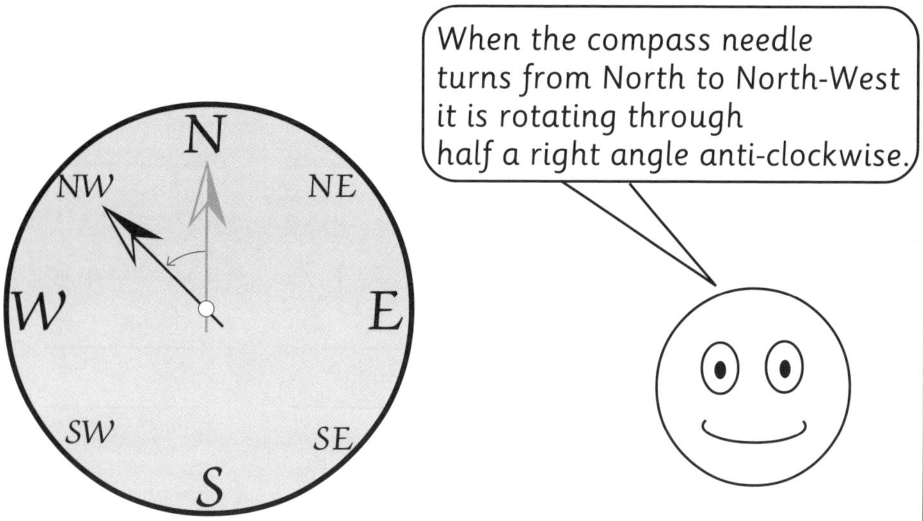


| | |
|---|---|
| (a) If the compass needle is pointing West and then turns half a right angle anti-clockwise, in which direction will it point? | |
| (b) If the compass needle is pointing South-East and then turns half a right angle clockwise, in which direction will it point? | |

Useful information:

When the needle turns through a right angle we say that it turns through 90 degrees.
We can write 90 degrees like this: 90°

## Mental Speed

How quickly can you answer these questions?
Time yourself and record your score.

1) 12 ÷ 3 =

2) 49 ÷ 7 =

3) 36 ÷ 6 =

4) 40 ÷ 8 =

5) 12 ÷ 2 =

6) 54 ÷ 6 =

7) 27 ÷ 9 =

8) 27 ÷ 3 =

9) 42 ÷ 6 =

10) 81 ÷ 9 =

11) 64 ÷ 8 =

12) 28 ÷ 4 =

13) 50 ÷ 5 =

14) 30 ÷ 6 =

15) 72 ÷ 8 =

16) 20 ÷ 4 =

17) 36 ÷ 9 =

18) 28 ÷ 7 =

19) 72 ÷ 9 =

20) 24 ÷ 6 =

Time taken:

☐ minutes and

☐ seconds.

# Mixed Number Practice Page

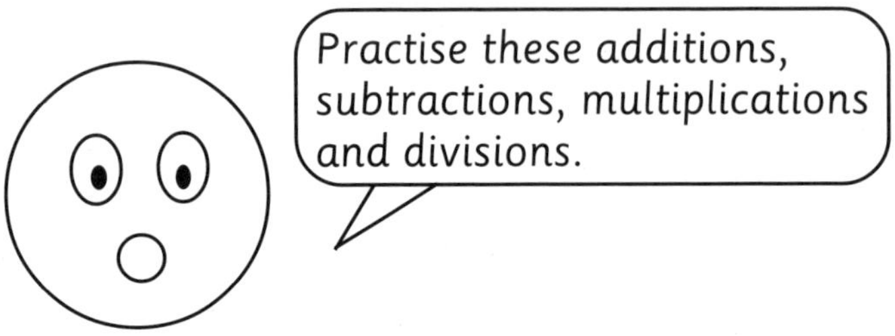


| | | | | |
|---|---|---|---|---|
| (a) 649 + 87 | (b) 519 + 285 | (c) 199 + 199 | (d) 775 + 25 | (e) 425 + 275 |
| (f) 648 - 135 | (g) 917 - 456 | (h) 723 - 386 | (i) 800 - 72 | (j) 909 - 186 |
| (k) 25 x 3 | (l) 19 x 4 | (m) 20 x 4 | (n) 17 x 5 | (o) 48 x 2 |
| (p) 8)48 | (q) 6)39 | (r) 4)28 | (s) 3)22 | (t) 5)30 |